SUCCESSFUL
EXPANSION
for the Small Busi

SUCCESSFUL EXPANSION
for the Small Business
The Daily Telegraph Guide

M J Morris

Kogan Page

To Carole and Nell

Copyright ©M J Morris 1984

All rights reserved

First published in Great Britain in 1984
by Kogan Page Ltd, 120 Pentonville Road, London N1 9JN

British Library Cataloguing in Publication Data
Morris, Michael John
   Successful expansion for the small business.
   1. Small business — Great Britain —
   Management
   I. Title
   658'.022'0941 HD62.7

ISBN 0-85038-822-8
ISBN 0-85038-823-6 Pbk

Printed by Billing & Sons Limited, Worcester.

Contents

Foreword 7
by David Davenport, DL, Chairman of the Council for Small Industries in Rural Areas

Chapter 1 What Expansion Involves 9
Why firms expand and how 10; The prize to be won and the price to be paid 13; Riding the tiger 17; Conclusion 19

Chapter 2 People 21
Attitudes to work 22; The working environment 24; Industrial psychology 26; The fair boss 29; Finding good people 30; Keeping good people 33; Keeping control 35; Systems and people 37; The boss controlling his own activity 38

Chapter 3 Strategic Planning for Results 41
Elements of the plan 42; Putting the plan together 50

Chapter 4 Keeping on Course 51
Management control 51; Management accounting 52; What needs to be controlled 55

Chapter 5 Advice and Advisers 64
Banks 66; Advice agencies 67; Business consultants 67; Consultants as decision makers 68; Staff attitudes to consultants 69; Sources of advice 70

Chapter 6 More of the Same, or Exciting New Products? 75
Existing products, present markets 75; New products, new markets 76; New product, present markets 77; Ways and means 79; New products for old 83

Chapter 7 Expanding by Takeover 88
What is on offer? 88; Identifying possible acquisitions 89; Putting competitors into business 90; Financial aspects 92; How to pay 95; Some of the traps 95; Blending old and new 96; Taxation and other liabilities 97

Chapter 8 New Products 98
Identifying customers' problems and needs 100; New product development budgeting 102; Government, and other help 103; Creative thinking 104; Other people's ideas 108; Patents 110

Chapter 9 Finance 111
Evaluating capital needs 113; Sources of finance 115; Relationships with lenders 119; Limited companies 120

Chapter 10 Production 122
Efficient production 125; Quality and its control 126; Systems 128; Purchasing 129; Safety 130; Premises 131

Appendix 1 Statistics in Management 133

Appendix 2 Financial Planning 136

Appendix 3 Business and the Law 143

Appendix 4 Useful Addresses and Information 148

Appendix 5 Further Reading 152

Index 155

Foreword

by David Davenport
Chairman of the Council for Small Industries in Rural Areas

Whilst working for growing firms and more recently as an adviser to them, Michael Morris has identified a real need. Numerous textbooks are available to assist the small businessman, in the main they deal with specific subjects, but in this one he brings together all those many considerations that must be weighed up by anyone contemplating expansion of their business.

Businessmen, be they manufacturers, shopkeepers, hoteliers, builders or others, can all benefit from the lessons discussed. The manager of an expanding small business very often has his own specialism, possibly learned when employed in a larger company, but it is essential for him to have at least a working knowledge of, and some expertise in all the main disciplines of management covering marketing, production, finance and above all, people. The task is very demanding, the risks are great, fortunes can be made or lost and the support and understanding of family and friends are vital.

At a time when, hopefully, the economy is on the road to recovery this comprehensively written book can only help encourage business expansion. Whether you are a manager of a small business possibly about to embark on expansion, a student of business studies at a university or college, or a central or local government adviser to small firms, I commend this manual to you.

Chapter 1
What Expansion Involves

In many quarters the popular picture of the small businessman is that he lacks something. The drive, the intelligence, some essential quality must be in short supply otherwise the business would be bigger and growing still. After all, every capitalist is greedy, isn't he?

This idea is given extra weight by economists who base many of their assumptions about the behaviour of human beings on predictions of what 'economic man' would do. Economic man is a dreary creature whose only motive for doing anything is gain, and whose ultimate ambition is to monopolise world trade. To make him even less like a human being he is portrayed as being prepared to move mountains for a net gain of pence. If there is money in something he will do it, and his choice of action will be dictated by the biggest profit. To be fair to economists they acknowledge that people are not really like that, but the idea has somehow become widespread without its essential rider that it provides no more than a rough guide to likely human behaviour. Since the number of people and the huge range of choices open to each one produces a more or less unpredictable scene, some simplification is vital if any forecasts are ever to be made, hence economic man. Dangers obviously lie in swallowing whole the intentional over-simplification as it stands. If other influences are added, such as left-wing ideas and over-exposure to certain board games based on a fantasy version of business life, it is easy to see how cynical or misguided ideas of business owners' motives are born.

Casual observation supported by academic research confirms that the majority of small firms do not wish to grow very much, if at all. To be sure, many would find some extra business very useful but not if it meant taking on lots of extra staff, bigger premises and more problems. Certainly only a very tiny minority would want to follow the example of Henry Ford or Clarence Birdseye and found massive, multinational dynasties. While very few have such vaunting ambitions many more would like to

SUCCESSFUL EXPANSION

expand to take advantage of market opportunities. Still more find themselves forced to expand to protect their existing business from potential competitors, to give customers a better service, to become big enough to employ management and take some of the load off the owner, or for any one of a hundred other reasons.

If the extra risks and work associated with expanding a business are accompanied by some material gain it seems only reasonable that the owner should be rewarded. Rarely, however, is an expansion motivated by profit considerations alone, hence the monopoly and greed theory of business people's motives has to be discarded as inadequate.

Why firms expand and how

The few people who expand their firms solely to make more money tend not to be among the ranks of the stupendously successful because an obsession with their own interests diverts attention from the real reason for the firm's existence. The only way in which a firm can exist long term is to have at heart its customers' interests, and to earn profits by serving them. Money is by no means unimportant. It is less pleasant to run an unprofitable firm than a profitable one, and in any case the firm's survival depends on healthy margins, positive cash flows and the availability of surpluses for reinvestment. But profit comes only as a reward for doing the main job well. The owner will rightly try to produce the best income, but he can do it only by satisfying his customers' real needs and constantly striving to get better at doing so. There are exceptions of course, particularly where a supplier has cornered the output of some essential or desirable commodity, but they are beyond the scope of this book. Even then the relationship with the customer can be abused only for a limited period of time, as the oil exporting countries are now finding.

SERVICE TO CUSTOMERS

The overwhelming majority of small firms to whom this book is addressed will find that they live or die according to the extent that they serve their customers. To expand, therefore, they either need more customers or need to sell more to existing customers, or perhaps some of each. To enable the firm to do either, the customers must be satisfied already with the firm's products and service or must believe that they will be.

WHAT EXPANSION INVOLVES

Most successful expansions of small firms have therefore been based on a value-for-money appeal supported by some assurance of quality. In the extremely successful cases it has also rested on some underlying sense of mission, a dream, a single-minded and rock-like determination to see that the customer is well served. However it is described, it has meant that the general standard of living has been raised and, as a planned side-effect, sizeable fortunes have been made.

If this begins to sound rather too fanciful, one example alone should suffice to prove its true hard-headedness — Marks & Spencer. There are plenty of others — Lego toys, Birds Eye frozen foods, Cadbury confectionery, Burberry rainwear, and dozens more.

Overseas readers who are unfamiliar with Marks & Spencer may like to know that it is the best-known and most trusted mass-retailing chain in Europe. It has 260-plus shops in most British towns and nine others in large European centres, apart from stores in other continents. Visitors to Britain flock to buy its underwear, clothing and knitwear which have a reputation for high quality at moderate prices. Its unadvertised 'St Michael' brand, the only one it stocks, is the leading UK maker of socks, trousers, underwear, bras, nightdresses and ladies' slips. Its attitude to quality control is formidable. Its staff are well trained, its stores are attractive, and its attention to detail is scrupulous. If a customer buys something that proves to be unsuitable, the refund will be given without question. In recent years it has added food products at very high prices and quality, with great success. A manufacturer who has a Marks & Spencer contract attracts admiration, envy, and pity. Admiration, because M&S are most careful about the firms they buy from, envy because orders are large and payment is prompt, pity because of the high standards that will be rigorously enforced on the supplier, including apparently irrelevant matters such as the way he treats his staff. All this started from a barrow in Leeds market in the late nineteenth century. In recent years Marks & Spencer have become very proud of their unbroken record of profits growth which they work very hard to maintain, but they know that it is their customers who provide it. Their guiding ideal is that last week's customers owe them absolutely nothing — if they are to get them back again they must be sure that they deserve custom through constant efforts to offer better, more attractive products and give continuously improving value.

SUCCESSFUL EXPANSION

In the hurly-burly of running a small business it may seem unrealistic to suggest that guiding principles can be stuck to so firmly. All that can be said in reply is that the real commercial geniuses like Marks & Spencer did, became very big, and still do. Likewise, the idea of comparing a very small firm with a giant may seem far-fetched. Is it really, though? All any potential customer is looking for is a product that fits his needs, and Marks & Spencer have managed to do exactly that better than any competitor. Whether dealing with one customer or millions, small firm or large, it is a very important ingredient in any recipe for success. But it needs to be applied constantly and consistently.

It is worth comparing the trust, automatic by now, that a Marks & Spencer, a Lego, or any of their peers inspires, with the suspicion and cynicism that some other suppliers attract. Some firms are so keen to snatch as much profit as they can that they whittle and pare down the value they offer until it almost disappears. In the short term they can produce good financial results but customers are not stupid, and eventually desert to competitors who treat them better; or perhaps the treatment is the same but the new supplier possesses the somewhat minimal virtue of being different. An example of a few years ago was the mass production part of the British motor industry. Those firms which cynically offered substandard products to a home market where prices were among the world's highest made money for a time, but eventually massive desertions to imported cars brought the industry to its knees. It need not have happened, but they may now be learning. Recently, one British car maker had quality worries, and announced the revolutionary new idea of checking the quality of bought-in parts. Had I been their publicity man I would have wanted to suppress the slightest suggestion that they had ever done otherwise. But it has apparently had the desirable and scarcely surprising effect of improving reliability, so there may be hope for the industry yet. The point is that the car manufacturers started with the same clean slate as Lego or Marks & Spencer. One group is now trusted and liked, the other disliked and mistrusted; one might ask oneself, who finds it easier to sell? The sole cause in each case was the industry's own behaviour. This carries a powerful lesson for all organisations and institutions, but especially for the small business with ambitions.

REASONS FOR EXPANSION

While customer satisfaction may be the guiding light of the expanding firm, the reasons for undertaking expansion are often mixed. They include:

- Increasing the firm's security through greater size
- Testing and proving management and product ideas
- Personal satisfaction of seeing something grow
- Giving career prospects to staff
- Building something for the owner's children
- Bringing greater technical excellence to a particular field
- Making bought-in items in-house, usually to increase reliability but sometimes to reduce cost.

Some of these carry obvious dangers. If the firm is being built up for children, there must be some certainty that they will want to become involved. The picture looks very different as between a 40-year old with a 20-year old heir, and a 45-year old whose child is only five. If the child decides to join the family firm, he should be encouraged to make his own way in life before doing so. Ideally, he would work elsewhere in a firm with a reputation for excellence in a similar industry, learning best practice and getting the feeling of what responsibilities are like (and making youthful mistakes out of sight of Dad) until 25 or 30. When he eventually joins the business he will have an independence of mind and different perspectives to complement those of his parent, and would inject current thinking into a business that might just be about to run out of ideas. This is preferable to those tragic instances of children leaving education and immediately joining the family firm, becoming third-rate imitators of their parent's outdated attitudes, but lacking his saving experience and canniness. Too often the firm fails when they have reached middle life, and they find themselves unemployed and unemployable at the age of 50.

Likewise, the wish to improve technical excellence should not be pursued for its own sake but only if the customer really wants it enough to pay for it. What might be called the Concorde syndrome seems to afflict engineering firms in particular.

The prize to be won and the price to be paid

Since time out of mind the rich merchant's wealth has been envied. The possibility of rags-to-riches progress from poor apprentice to wealth and social success as Lord Mayor of

SUCCESSFUL EXPANSION

London is part of our heritage — every British child is told the story of Dick Whittington. The chance for the ordinary person to make a fortune was widened immeasurably by the industrial revolution, an opportunity taken by many people regardless of social origins or educational attainments. Successful business people also have considerable standing in the community. They are looked up to and admired, not only for their wealth, but also for their effectiveness in their chosen way of life, implying as it does an ability to stand alone, take on complex and challenging tasks and win.

THE OWNER'S SITUATION

Most onlookers are well aware of the prizes that commercial success can bring, but very few know what sacrifices are made along the way. Being already involved in business, the owner contemplating expansion knows all about the long hours, the stress, and the absence of any normal social life. As the business expands these pressures will be accentuated. It may be dangerous to assume that achieving a goal means that a rest can be taken. For one thing, striving for growth seems to be habit-forming; no sooner is one target reached than the next is being pursued. For another, while the nature of the owner's job will change as the firm grows, it is unlikely that he will work any less hard.

That change in the owner's job is central to the firm's ability to grow successfully. The boss will have to stop doing many things himself and learn how to get work done by other people. They will never do it as well or as quickly as he can, but only in crises should he take the job back and do it himself. Getting an increasing number of people to work as closely as possible to the time and quality standards he sets himself, and keeping it up, is one of the biggest challenges facing the owner. Making that transition from 'doer' to 'manager of doers' is a leap that many business people never make, with the consequence that they are forever furious at their employees' incompetence, their employees are constantly fed up with them, and the firm's potential growth is stunted.

Having lost his direct involvement with many day-to-day details, the owner will almost certainly feel out of touch with events, and suspect that the firm is drifting out of control. That brings him up against another principle of sound management: the need not only to allocate work to others, but to be in control of it. To do this he will need systems for recording and reporting on events, and probably a certain amount of paperwork. For many practical people running firms, paperwork is like poison, but the manager of the expanding firm cannot avoid it. Even if the control systems are not on paper but are being run on a small computer, the owner will still be confronted by information in the form of figures with which he must be completely familiar and at ease.

The intentional relinquishing by the owner of personal control over important but minor actions is necessary because time has to be freed for the matters that only he can and must tackle. That is not to say, by any means, that he ignores all detail, but that he deals with only the minimum necessary at all times.

Early in his expansion the owner will have to lead forcefully. The growth of the firm will mean that he gathers a team about him, of which he becomes the leader who encourages, rather than orders. If he is to inspire his staff to perform well, they must feel free to some extent to do the job their way. The effective boss will show an interest in their methods, and help them to eradicate shortcomings, building on their strengths. He will seek the employees' ideas, perhaps nudging them towards a solution if need be, but never imposing his thoughts except as an unavoidable final resort. Thus he will eventually become more like a very demanding teacher developing a pupil's ability to think for himself, than a sergeant bellowing orders. The sergeant's approach is needed in the early stages, but it will work long term only in a firm where staff will never need to develop their own skills to deal with the growing demands of their jobs. It can work in the expanding firm for a time, but falls down the moment that the intimidated employees meet a crisis while their tin god is unavailable. In the early stages of growth the firm looks like a dictatorship. Later, as it grows, it may look more like a democracy, but it will still be led by one person, and tightly controlled by him.

Health and stress
Undoubtedly the sergeant's approach is easier for many business owners. Being forced to allow other people a little freedom, accepting their different methods, acting like a teacher, all these cause more stress for the owner, whose drives and anxieties naturally make him seek superhuman performance from his all-too-fallible staff. We all need some stress to keep us alive and some people thrive on a great deal of it and live to a great old age after leading the most challenging lives. Others are affected

by even slight amounts of stress, constantly catching colds and other minor ailments, being unable to concentrate, and eventually developing more grave stress-related disease. Most of us are at neither extreme, but knowing his capacity for stress is important to the owner of a firm. Running any small business is fraught enough with responsibility, but one that is trying to expand makes even greater demands. Another thing rarely understood by wage- and salary-earners is the commitment of all the family's assets to the bank to cover the firm's borrowings. Thus, failure of the business almost certainly means personal financial ruin for the owners.

It therefore makes excellent sense to talk to one's spouse before deciding to take on an extra load of responsibility. This is suggested for two reasons: because they know the owner really well, and can usually be trusted for the most concerned and informed judgement and advice; and because they have to bear the burden of being virtually a one-parent family with a breadwinner who, when he is not away, comes home just to eat, sleep and wash.

Another person to consult is the family doctor. He sees a lot of people broken by stress, not all of them business owners, just people who took on more than they could manage. The doctor is running a small firm too, and fully understands how there is always more to do than can reasonably be done. His value is increased by his personal awareness of the effects of stress, for GPs themselves suffer from more than the average rate of stress-related illness. On top of that, he has the technical knowledge of how to deal with it.

Despite these worthy precautions, even the fittest, least unhealthily-stressed business owner will fall ill sometimes. Such is their admirable optimism, the attitude of most small businessmen to illness is that it is something that happens to other people. The effects on the business and the family of sickness and death are matters to discuss with a good insurance broker. As a general rule, at least two types of cover are advisable: to save the firm from failing, and to give the family some sort of income. Everyone's circumstances are different, but few firms could carry a boss who became seriously and permanently disabled, so appropriate insurances should be taken out. If the worst happened and the owner died suddenly, it would be a godsend to receive a cheque for (say) £50,000, which could pay for quite a lot of highly professional consultant's time to tide the firm over the crisis. Likewise, the owner and his family could take out their own cover to assure them of a permanent income if he could no longer work. Even if the firm were able to look after them for a time, there has to be a limit to its ability to carry expensive passengers.

Family support
Supporting his family is one of the owner's main responsibilities in life. To enable him to discharge it effectively he needs *their* support. This is especially true in the expanding firm. While contented Mr Smith manages to snatch a Sunday off occasionally to go out with his family, ambitious Mr Brown is at a trade fair in Birmingham, entertaining a buyer in Scotland, catching up on work at the office, or driving to the airport to catch a plane. He might give up his Sunday to travel, so as to do some work with the local agent in his hotel and get a good night's sleep before a crucial meeting on Monday morning. Wives or husbands prepared to put up with this willingly are rare creatures. As most of us are less than perfect, it is perhaps only fair to explain to the spouse involved the truth about the 100-hour working week. They will be very lonely, they will need to invent their own entertainments when the owner is away, the family home will be expected to be a showplace in apple-pie order at all times for the social side of business, dinner parties will be sprung at short notice, baby-sitters will be in demand to cover the sudden trip to London for business entertainment (personal grooming must always be in a perfect state for the same reason), and when all this effort has been put in, the tycoon arrives home with a pile of dirty washing and falls asleep. Before anyone in the family can talk to him he is off early in the morning leaving only a note showing the coming week's travels.

It takes a very special sort of person, hugely dedicated to the firm's success, to put up with such demands and this sort of treatment. It is important, therefore, to remember this loyalty, and constantly to show that it is appreciated very much indeed. The evening phone call home from the hotel, the present from an overseas trip, the genuine and sincere efforts to reciprocate, are vital.

Riding the tiger
As plenty of well-known examples prove, in one lifetime a successful firm can be established, built up, and grow to an

international scale. Other firms take longer, perhaps several generations, to develop to the same size. They may be in completely different industries and run in completely different ways, but the characteristics they must have in common to be confident of survival are:

- Access to adequate funds
- Proper control over and protection of assets
- Keeping enough cash available
- Competent, motivated staff
- Satisfactory influence over and responsiveness to present and future markets
- Appropriate levels of costs.

It is top management's job to ensure that all these essentials are present all the time. Apart from ensuring that the company keeps within the law, there is not much else for the owner to worry about. Put like that, it sounds fairly simple, so why all the fuss? Because it is an over-simplification, akin to saying that maintenance of human life requires only health, sustenance, oxygen, warmth and shelter.

The statement as it stands is true, but is nonetheless only the starting point of more complex matters. It is not useless, for a clear understanding of what the necessities are is itself necessary, but one needs to pursue the generalisation to see how it is to be brought about. Access to adequate funds, for example, involves estimating the current and future need for funds and in turn knowing costs and payment terms, market forecasts and hence sales forecasts; then assembling information on sources of funding and negotiating with them, possibly after taking professional advice; and constantly monitoring performance against the estimates originally made to identify irregularities and take corrective action.

That in itself is a fairly major task, but it is only one from a list of six, so it is easy to see that the owner's job is much more than a normal, full-time one. As the business progresses the chance may arise to employ professional managers to take over whole areas of direct responsibility from the owner. That can be a great relief, but it does not absolve the owner from involvement. As at earlier stages of the firm's development, he still has the ultimate, buck-stopping responsibility, but his relationship to it changes and his job becomes different. It still places great demands upon him, but the demands are not the same as before — once again, he is working through other people to get things done rather than doing them himself.

The load on him is unlikely to change, for other reasons. As the firm grows it is undertaking more transactions, making a bigger range of products, dealing with more customers. Also, the range of tasks being done by employees multiplies. For example, when the hotel and travel bill was £1500 per year, the odd 10 per cent that might have been due to misuse was hardly worth spending time to identify. By the time it has climbed to £100,000 annually, it is worth employing somebody who spends much of their time checking on claims. So a greater variety of work is done, as well as a greater volume, which means that there are more things to go wrong. If a fixed proportion of all the things the firm does always must reach the boss's desk, then the boss will be busier. Thus, the change in his job is not an isolated event, but is continuously evolving to ensure that he is able to keep on top of the unchanging essentials.

Further demands will be placed on his time by the need for the owner to coordinate departmental concerns in the interest of the firm as a whole. For instance, the sales manager may want lower prices, the financial director a price increase; the production manager may want to reduce the number of products, the marketing manager to introduce additional ones; all of them are right, in the sense that they will better achieve their objectives within the firm if the decision goes their way. But someone has to hold the ring, knocking heads together if need be, and make the final decision. Knowing that, whatever the decision is, it will displease some or even all of them, the owner has then to ensure that ruffled feelings are smoothed, forecasts of doom are not made to come true, and generally to see that the decision is carried through to improve the overall position of the company, as was intended.

Conclusion

If this sounds a far cry from the idea of running a nice little business, that is intentional. It is meant to emphasise the point made throughout this chapter, that the owner's job undergoes a radical change as the company grows. Beyond a certain point he will achieve results only through the efforts of other people, and his success or failure will depend largely on how good he is at recruiting the right people and getting the best out of them. To some, the challenge of making that change is exhilarating, to others, insurmountable. The whole question of people, including the owner, and getting results out of them, is dealt with in Chapter 2.

Chapter 2
People

Of all the resources in a firm its people are far and away the most important. Machines will not run themselves, at least not yet, and without human guidance, money left unused just lies there gathering dust. What gives them life and usefulness is people. Yet these amazingly gifted organisms are frequently undervalued or ignored, or at best given merely token recognition. In the typical annual report from a public company the chairman will report at length on new products, the research programme, exports, expansion plans and, of course, the financial results. Tucked away a few sentences from the end comes what seems to be a standard paragraph along these lines: 'Your board is sure that shareholders would wish to join them in thanking the staff for their hard work and dedication in what has been another difficult trading year.'

To some extent one must sympathise because there is no convenient way of expressing the effort that staff have made, no measure exists that can show people among the other assets on the balance sheet. It is certain that few chairmen of large companies spend as little time on consideration of matters to do with people as that brief reference in the annual report would suggest. They recognise that the increase, or decrease, in the company's wealth on which they are reporting has been caused by their people, and most will allocate their time accordingly.

There is a darker side to dealing with employees which the traditional financially-orientated report cannot show. The results of any firm will have been bought at a price, through the efforts and sacrifices of staff. For some the burden of performance will be too great, and will exact a toll measured in illness and premature death, broken marriages and alienation from children. The shareholder in the public company will know nothing of this but will get the financial benefits of it. The owner of the small firm also gets the benefits, but is close to the problems which are troubling people he knows personally and feels responsible for. It is obviously desirable that the owner of an expanding firm prepares himself for the load that will fall on his conscience if, or more likely when, some symptom of overwork hits one of his people. A certain mental and moral toughness is essential if that experience is not to get the boss down.

The firm is entitled to a fair day's work for a fair day's pay, so it is inevitable that demands will be made on people from time to time that they find difficult or uncomfortable to meet. One of the many differences between management and labour in the UK is the differing expectations that employers have of each. Whatever its rights and wrongs, the tradition is that labour is expected to work for a particular period in the day at or above a minimum intensity and within quality limits. Management is paid partly for those things but in addition and above all it is paid for results. This last part of the manager's contract usually leads to his working for many more than his contracted hours. The combination of time spent doing his full job, time not spent fulfilling family and social commitments, and worrying about both, is what places so much stress on the manager. There is also much stress on the shop-floor which has been studied extensively in large establishments such as car assembly plants, but it is by no means confined to them. Most of the reasons for stress on the shop-floor of the small firm can be laid at the door of management. Usually it arises through poor work scheduling, insufficient training, unclear or ambiguous orders, poor working conditions, or some such reason.

If he has any conscience the boss will not find it easy to live with some of the consequences of the demands he makes. If he has no conscience about it he will still see that small people in big jobs are ineffective, and will seek to reduce the risk of his people getting out of their depth.

The whole question of how to get the best out of people at work is far from being an exact science. Because it is also one of the most important problems facing the ambitious small firm, this chapter is necessarily long.

Attitudes to work

Many people fall into the trap of thinking that everyone wants more or less the same from their lives. If the small businessman makes that assumption about his fellow men he makes a great mistake. If it remains uncorrected it will lead to considerable misunderstanding and eventually to bitterness and alienation between owner and employees.

THE OWNER
Although there is no such thing as the typical owner of a small firm, a very high proportion of them share certain attitudes to their work, some of which are:

> The existence of the firm and the jobs it provides are secured only by service to customers.
> The job gets done properly whatever the personal inconvenience.
> There can be no passengers: all staff and assets must pull their weight.
> The owner knows best where the firm's best interests lie.
> Only good work should be paid for.
> The firm's and the employees' best interests are almost identical.
> Enterprise and risk-taking should be properly rewarded.

It is perfectly right and proper for the owner of a firm to hold such views for without them he would lack part of the engine that drives him and makes him an effective leader of other people. Nevertheless he will be wrong to assume that the staff share those values completely. It may be hard for employees to criticise them logically but that does not mean that they hold those views themselves. Logic is not utterly unimportant here but when people are forming their ideas all kinds of other influences come into play. Among those that are usually important are self-interest, feelings based on emotional and instinctive reactions, attitudes instilled in childhood, and the values of friends, workmates and neighbours.

THE EMPLOYEE
Any notion of a typical employee can be as misleading as that of a typical boss, but it may be worthwhile examining some commonly held attitudes to compare with the list above. Employees' ideas can include:

— The firm wants as much as it can get at the least cost.
— The harder employees work the richer the boss gets.
— The boss may work hard but his rewards are excessive.
— Work is unpleasant and to be avoided when possible, done at a comfortable rate, and dropped exactly on time.
— Leisure activities are more satisfying than work.

SUCCESSFUL EXPANSION

— The main reason for working is income and the chance to see your mates.
— Work can be done more quickly, but it is wiser to make it last.

This is, of course, a grotesque caricature but it may contain more than a grain of truth. Highly-motivated staff do undoubtedly exist particularly among skilled categories, and most employees would acknowledge that their jobs depend on the firm's commercial success or at least on it not failing. At the same time it would be as foolish to ignore the propensity for cynicism among staff as to overlook the possibility that they might be proud to work for a firm showing all the outward signs of prosperity, one of which might be a boss who drives an expensive car. People are complicated creatures who can be both thrilled by new equipment to work with and capable of complaining about the way they have been exploited to make the purchase possible. Thus the boss who approaches an employee to seek cooperation that he firmly believes to be in everyone's interest can be baffled and exasperated by a negative and obstructive response. Yet on another occasion this difficult employee could be as helpful as one could wish.

These mismatches between different ways of seeing the world have caused such deep frustration that some owners have even given up their businesses altogether. 'You can't deal with these trouble-makers, they're crazy, don't know what's good for them. They spend more time arguing and having meetings among themselves than working to pay their wages' — these are the sort of furious and uncomprehending remarks such owners make. Yet these apparently suicidal employees seem quite normal away from the work place and not a bit like heralds of the red revolution. It is just possible that they are bent on destroying the economy of the western world, but statistically unlikely. More probably the boss is failing to face up to the fact that the staff see him as unreasonable and difficult.

The working environment

The entire question of the effective use of people has so much significance for firms of all sizes, and indeed for whole economies, that academics as well as managers have made great efforts to come to grips with it. One cheering conclusion for the small firm is that the worst troubles seem to occur in the largest units. In small firms the relationship between the management and its employees is more personal so that any difficulties are usually cleared up quickly and face-to-face. Also the staff can see in a small firm a clear relationship between what they do and the customer's requirements, which adds to the common ground between them and the owner. Often the boss himself works on the shop-floor, creating a sense of solidarity and team effort as well as enabling him to set an example of high standards of performance.

The warning that these studies contain for the growing firm are centred on its inevitable tendency to import big-firm problems with its expansion. In the big firm impersonal dealings mean that the employee cannot get his problems and reasonable complaints dealt with — the foreman shrugs his shoulders, privately agrees but says it is all due to 'them up there'. So instead of concentrating on his job he concentrates on his grievance and the unreasonableness of bosses. Furthermore, he feels he is little more than a number on a clock-card rather than a human being, easily replaceable by someone else with similar skills and attributes. That view is strengthened by the way in which so many jobs in larger firms have become highly specialised.

In a small factory one man may get a lot of welcome variety in his work as the limited number of people often means that everyone has to be versatile. As firms grow, greater specialisation will probably creep in until the ultimate position is reached where a man spends an entire working life inserting windscreens on a car assembly line. Robotics will no doubt invalidate that particular example completely in the near future but for the time being it holds true, and is truer the lower the worker's skills are.

A further feature of the big plant is the employee who is virtually a passenger. Among large numbers one person can go unnoticed. Others seeing his example wonder why they should make any effort, and gradually the whole tempo can slow down. The idea can easily get about that the firm will survive however little effort one person makes, because the contribution of the individual is proportionally so small. Their distance from the customer means that commercial reality does not intrude, so the only brake on this pernicious process is any that the management may care to apply.

The expanding firm is unlikely to encounter all of these problems all at once. That does not justify ignoring them altogether, for they start to creep in imperceptibly at first. By the time they have gained a hold it will take a lot of time and effort even to make a start on reducing, let alone eradicating, them. It is better to head them off before they attack than to await clear evidence that they are established.

There is a range of symptoms: output per head and other indicators of productive efficiency will fall. Setting-up times will rise as will scrap rates, rework, absenteeism, self-certified sickness and staff turnover. Delivery times will lengthen, quality will fall and a less cooperative attitude will be generally apparent. Evidence of these disturbing changes will be difficult to spot because they will be partly masked by the normal and inevitable inefficiencies which are part of the usual pattern of things. By the time they are clearly visible in their own right they will be well entrenched and serious. Anyone who thinks this could not take place in his firm, even in its expanded form, should consider soberly the fog of explanations given for the occasional substandard performance at present. Sometimes the cold weather will be to blame, at others the hot; or difficulties with adjusting to the variety of short runs, or boredom with long runs; or any other pair of plausible but contradictory explanations. They are, of course, credible and they might even be the true causes. But if it is difficult to get to the bottom of normal events the abnormal will be that much more obscure. If the basic problems of growth have not been foreseen and banished before their appearance they could become irremovably ensconced, eating away invisibly at the foundations of the firm.

Industrial psychology

Industry has provided psychologists with important and fascinating areas of study, and psychology has in turn given managers many insights into the complex question of how and why people perform the way they do.

The psychologists who have made the greatest impact recently on industrialists' ideas of dealing with the work-force have tended to start not from what the bosses want but from the attitudes of the employees. They have looked at the needs which people want to satisfy before they are prepared to make an effort, and at the sort of handling to which they respond. Much of this work seems to reflect the views current in society, which is scarcely surprising, but it does provide a solid base of evidence from observation and research to support the various theories. It is therefore worth looking briefly at the more important ones.

Overall they break down into the theories that see work as unpleasant and something that employees will seek to avoid, and those who feel that work gives people chances for self-expression which they will gladly take if the right conditions are created. They were neatly identified as 'Theory X' and 'Theory Y' respectively by Professor Douglas McGregor.

Theory X was the principle on which most organisations had worked from the beginning of time until the 1950s. There were, of course, notable exceptions throughout history, but Theory X was predominant. People knew their place and kept to it, put up with unsavoury conditions and kept their mouths shut. They recognised the owner's legal right to manage, though major challenges to it were mounted from time to time. The power of the owner was so often misused that the inevitable reaction led to the creation of revolutionary socialism, trade unions and other movements which felt that there must be a better way of running things, and sometimes expressed that view violently. In favour of Theory X it could be said to be simple, clear and easy to understand. One either did what the boss wanted or one left, there being little room for compromise. The police and the military are the obvious examples of organisations with a strong foundation in the principle of Theory X, even though the latter have modified their methods considerably since the days when men died under the lash for what we today would regard as trivial offences. They, too, have discovered the modern school of management.

The industrial revolution made men grope for ways of controlling the sprawling business empires that were being created. The only large organisations from which they could draw contemporary lessons were the military and the church. Building on those examples there evolved the school of so-called 'scientific management'. Its underlying view of organisations was they they were very like machines. If people of the correct specification were connected up in the right way, the machine would do the bidding of its master. The man at the top knows best and hands down his instructions through clear lines of command to employees who execute them, and feed information back up the line about what they have done. The legacy of that school of thought can be seen in the fact that most chief executives would love to exercise the tight control over their organisations that it implies, as well as in the pyramid-shaped organisation chart that most use to describe how their responsibilities are discharged.

About half-way through the twentieth century social psychologists spoke up. They saw that tightness of control was not itself a guarantee of outstanding commercial performance. Often autocratically run organisations performed poorly, and they began to look for the reasons. They concluded that the view of an employee as a cog in a machine encouraged him to deliver no more than his labour, and grudgingly at that. A series of observations and experiments at a large electrical manufacturing firm in the USA came up with two main findings: people want some say in how they organise their work, and work better when it is allowed them; and that they will work only as hard as they feel their colleagues would like them to work. Thus two holes were blown in the then current ideas on how best to control a work-force. It could *not* pay to drive and strongly motivate people for they would almost always work within their workmates' norm. It *could* pay to take off some of the tight control and let people help to determine their own working patterns and methods. This theory grew in importance until it formed the 'human relations' school of management.

At much the same time, A H Maslow developed the idea that modern industrial man does not work for money alone, but for all sorts of other reasons. As primitive man moved towards the present day, the idea ran, the process of socialisation followed a pattern. Once the most basic needs for shelter, food, water, air, sleep and sex were satisfied, man set about obtaining safety from the many outside threats to his existence. Once that need was dealt with he looked for love and esteem and finally for some way of expressing himself as a complete human being. In our society today most people have the wherewithal to satisfy their most basic needs, the argument continues, and look for satisfaction of their higher needs. If they are disappointed in that, people will be dissatisfied and morale and quality of work will suffer.

Another worker in the field was Frederick Herzberg. His research led him to the view that the conditions under which people work can be divided into two distinct categories. 'Conditions' here means everything bearing on the working environment in the widest sense. The categories are, first, the matters that do not motivate if they are present but cause trouble if they are absent, and second, the factors that directly motivate people to work better. In the first category might be things like the state of the canteen, where cleanliness is expected but does not encourage greater efforts, and in the second are satisfactions of the higher needs through conferment of recognition of the individual's contribution and offering him some say in how he does his work.

These, then, are some of the main ideas, brutally paraphrased, which have formed management opinions of how people can be encouraged to give of their best. It is almost an entire academic discipline in itself, with much elaboration on these basic themes. The growing firm should recognise that it is an area fraught with difficulty and deserving commensurate attention.

To bring this brief historical sketch up to date it remains only to add that the pressures of recession during the last few years have added a further twist to the story. Faced by the tough realities of falling demand, rising costs and more unpredictable trading conditions, many managements have felt that their earlier concentration on human relations was no longer wholly appropriate. To add to the pressure, fewer managers are now employed, leaving those in jobs with less time than ever to consider their employees' higher needs. Rising unemployment has also made employees perhaps more ready to accept decisions about work practices in which they have no say. Thus the conditions seem right for a reassertion of authoritarian styles of management.

If any one single thing is clear from the foregoing it is that there is no one, single, standard approach known to work in all conditions. Probably the best advice that can be given is to learn from the achievements and mistakes of others and to evolve one's own, unique style which is a reflection of the personality with which one is blessed and the values one holds dear. It is as big a mistake to be too soft in dealing with employees as to be too hard, so flexibility and that uncommon attribute, common sense, will be called for. Personal prejudices should be muffled as far as possible so that in exercising his proper authority the boss discharges the full range of his responsibilities to the firm and its staff.

The fair boss

Every employer probably believes quite sincerely that he treats his work-force fairly, even when it is patently untrue. To guard oneself from this delusion it is helpful to consider not only the viewpoint of the boss but also that of the other person involved, the employee.

When an employee is judging the fairness or otherwise of the boss he looks above all else for consistency and integrity. If work begins at 8.30 everyone starts at that time, office staff and boss included. If office staff get clean lavatories so do factory staff, and so on. These and numerous other matters show everyone that all are treated equally and that there are no favourites. The only distinction between shop-floor and management is that mentioned previously, that managers are paid to get results in addition to delivering a day's attendance at their desks, so earning their higher incomes.

As for integrity, it is wise policy for the boss to be, and to be seen to be, honest in his dealings whether with staff or outsiders. If the boss sets the example by cheating a supplier he can scarcely complain if employees treat his time and property as fair game. The practical wisdom of this is very clear to anyone defending a charge of unfair dismissal from an employee fired for dishonesty. If that employee is charged by the police and tried in court, defence evidence of the dishonesties practised by the owner would be more embarrassing still.

An important element in fair dealings is compliance with all aspects of the law relating to employment. There is no reason why any small business owner should be expert in that or any other legal field. The various advice agencies dealing with small firms can take the firm's individual policy and turn it into the written documents the law requires, usually for a modest fee, and at very much less cost than that of a solicitor's services at an industrial tribunal.

Finding good people

Once again a systematic approach is more likely to yield successful results than are haphazard methods. The golf club grapevine might throw up the right recruit but it would be risky to use it as the sole publicity medium.

To start with, a note should be drawn up describing the job. These job descriptions will already be a standard feature of any firm that has taken proper advice on its personnel practices, one of their chief uses being to help identify who is responsible for doing what throughout the firm. It should state:

- ☐ The responsibilities of the jobholder
- ☐ The types of work he/she is expected to perform

PEOPLE

- ☐ The post to which the jobholder reports
- ☐ Which posts, if any, report to the jobholder.

Once the job description has drawn up the demands of the post, the next step is to specify the ideal candidate to fill it. In most matters some latitude should be allowed on either side of perfection to take account of the vagaries of real life, although if an absolute minimum qualification is mandatory it should be made clear that it is so. In preparing the specification the personalities of those with whom the new person will work have to be considered, as will any future promotion plans for him, in addition to the obvious question of his technical qualifications for the job. This procedure need not be long-winded but it is a useful precaution against contradictions in the owner's thinking and omissions of important matters. It is unlikely that anyone's reputation would be enhanced by announcing one week that a 25-year-old was being sought only to change it the next to a 45-year-old when all the interviewees turned out to be a bit too inexperienced.

It is advisable to follow this process even if the obvious candidate already works for the firm. To compare him with the specification for the ideal candidate can cause the owner to give some thought to what might otherwise be a purely instinctive decision, and therefore possibly a dangerous one. Once taken, the decision to promote good old Fred is virtually irrevocable. It is therefore worth making as sure as possible that he is the right man for the job before he and his wife celebrate. What to do about faithful Fred if he is passed over for what he thinks is his rightful promotion is another sort of problem which we come to later.

Now the job is ready to be advertised and how to do this will have to be decided. Should a recruitment agency be used to produce a shortlist or should the company advertise for direct applications? If it is to advertise, what style of ad, where is it to appear, when and how often? For staff likely to be found locally these questions scarcely need considering, for past experience and local knowledge, perhaps aided by the Jobcentre, will tell it what to do. But when a post of some responsibility is being offered it might be worth thinking about getting wider coverage than the local media can give. Some surprisingly good people may be available only 30 miles away, beyond the local paper's reach but prepared to commute daily. Others may be prepared to move from another part of the country because of poor prospects where they are and some may actively welcome a move for family reasons. It would be foolish to discount these people if they could be reached at acceptable cost through an ad in a professional magazine or a widely read national newspaper.

Recruitment agencies can advertise a job, process applications and hold initial screening interviews to assemble a shortlist for the employer to meet. Some carry a list of job-seekers whom they try to match to incoming vacancies. Most of those with lists specialise in a particular area of employment such as engineering, selling or plastics. They can usually be found advertising in the appropriate professional magazines. Often the different functions are available from one firm, and it is worth the owner's while to enquire where the main strength of each consultant lies and relate it to his own needs and expectations. He should certainly brace himself for a big bill if he does use their services. It is an advertising- and labour-intensive business, neither of which comes cheap. It can be argued that it would be money well spent in keeping the owner at arm's length from the time-consuming drudgery of the early stages of the recruitment process. The counter-argument is that the decision is such a vital one for the client in the early period of his expansion that he must not allow another person to get between him and his potential employee, possibly filtering out the person who is not the best candidate on paper but who is exactly right for the team. Recruitment is partly a logical process but it also must involve instincts and feelings. If it did not most jobs could be filled from application forms alone. The interview is rightly important in our minds because it is then that we see, or think we see, the person in the round for the first time. Only then can the process really begin of weighing the different qualifications and qualities of candidates to produce a list ranked in order of preference. Only the owner can carry out that process, and to do it as well as it can be done he needs to see all interviewees. Ideally, that is what he will do but the other pressures on his time may well force him to accept a less than perfectionist approach, as in so many aspects of his business life.

It is advisable to interview more than once before a final decision is made, and also for interviewers to work in pairs and compare notes. The recruitment consultant will be happy to help at a price, or one of the small-firms agencies might produce someone suitable. Interviews are not easy even for professionals, and the amateur risks being hoodwinked by the better actors among the candidates. If a consultant is to be used he should be allowed to make the fullest contribution of which he is capable, especially where the recruitment of senior staff is concerned. He should be engaged at the start of the project, assisting at even the earliest stage when the need for the new appointment is being discussed. More on the subject of consultants and advisers generally appear in Chapter 5.

Keeping good people

Once he has found good staff the owner's mind will immediately turn to means of keeping them. There will always be disappointments when key employees suddenly announce that they are off, sometimes for reasons quite beyond the owner's control. The best that can be hoped for is that nobody whom the firm wishes to keep ever leaves because of the owner's actions or inaction.

It is important to keep the team together for as long as possible, once it is working well, because losing good members of it can be disruptive and costly. There are the obvious costs of advertising and the loss of productive time spent interviewing, but also less visible costs associated with the time the new man will spend in acclimatisation before he starts to pull his full weight. On top of that there is the risk that the departing employee may set up a rival business or join a competitor, taking customers with him. (One of the most fertile seed-beds for new firms is existing small firms, where employees see much of what goes into running a business and think they could do at least as well.)

Incentive schemes are often considered as a means of attracting and holding on to staff. They should be installed only after a full appreciation has been gained of their possible implications. In most small businesses there is not enough management time available to operate permanent incentives. An annual bonus is paid over too long a span of time to motivate most people's day-to-day performance; a weekly or monthly reward takes a lot of calculating; to be really effective it must work on the key performance required of each individual, which can be complex to set up and lead to people ignoring important parts of their work on which bonus is not paid; and to cap it all there are the rows about whose fault the substandard performance was — production stopped because materials ran out or the machine broke down — so the denial of bonus was unfair. It is quite possible to find that the firm pays out money on bonuses for no visible return except to attract ill-feeling, which was not the original intention.

Just as the best fertiliser is the farmer's boot, the best incentive scheme may well be to pay people highly and keep their performance up to the mark by good quality supervision at shop-floor level and the frequent presence among the staff of top managers. The owner of the growing firm may have acquired an office away from the noise of the shop-floor, but he needs to keep a keen interest in what is going on. As the firm grows he will need to gauge progress less and less by glancing at the size of that day's heap of finished goods and increasingly by the paper reports from supervisors, but he must still keep his finger on the pulse of the real activity that the figures represent. To take the production department as an example, not a day should pass without the boss being seen on the shop floor. His visit will not be just for verbally patting the workers on the head but for sound, businesslike reasons. He can gain valuable up-to-date information with his own eyes, and his interest and involvement will keep everyone on their toes. Invariably his first contact should be with the person in charge, otherwise the impression could be given that the old man spies on managers behind their backs. Mere ownership of the factory does not absolve anyone from the obligation to observe life's little courtesies. Staff will be nervous and pleased to see the owner and keen to show off their best work. A little appreciation and charm go a long way, as does praise for satisfactory work. If someone's work is not good enough the owner should respect the dignity of his manager by not trying to sort out the problem himself, and keeping any criticisms for a private talk with the manager concerned. He must not try to buy popularity by blanket admiration of everything, bad work included, or else his manager will face an insuperable problem in trying to raise standards — it was good enough for the boss, after all. Intelligently and sincerely made, these efforts will not only yield information but establish the boss as a personality to people who might not otherwise meet him, create more of a team spirit and help the production manager strengthen his authority and gain in confidence.

Frequent visits to departments enable not only present performance to be observed but also opportunities for improved methods to be considered. More effective methods and new machines and equipment can be good motivators in themselves.

Even if the introduction of such novelties is irrelevant the boss can also watch out for deterioration in working conditions. Some of them are controlled by law but others merely reflect the attitude of management to the people it employs. A work place that is clean and well lit tells the staff how the firm feels about them just as, in its own way, a filthy, unsafe working environment does. If good working conditions are provided the management can reasonably require staff to contribute to the general cleanliness and tidiness, and thus to safety and efficiency. One of the biggest surprises the author has ever had was on visiting a five-year-old plastic moulding factory in the USA. It was as clean as on the day it opened. The staff wore everyday leisure clothes which did not get dirty as they kept their machines so clean. In many similar factories in Britain the floors are littered with scrap and waste, gangways are blocked by old cardboard boxes and sacks of plastic, machines are dirty and work stations covered in grime, and spilt plastic granules crunch underfoot. No doubt there are as good factories in Britain as in the USA, and doubtless all USA practice is not to those standards, but there is absolutely no reason why a workshop cannot be kept clean, and sound reasons why it should be. Neither set of conditions happened by accident but both were caused, one by management resolution and the other by management neglect.

Keeping control

Some people think that being a boss means a constant and unrelieved diet of decision-making. No sooner is one cleared out of the way than the next arrives, then the one following, in an unbroken flow throughout the working year. What is not so well understood is that a decision taken is not yet a decision implemented, and that attached to each decision are consequences, some of which can be unpleasant. Some of the most painful decisions are those relating to people.

On page 31 the suitability of faithful old Fred was being considered for the new job of production manager. Fred had been with the firm for the whole decade of its existence, having given up a secure job to help to start it up. He has worked through three Christmases as well as innumerable weekends and nights to deal with crises, all without complaint. Once he even took no pay for three months to help the firm through a difficult period in the early days. As shop foreman he has

SUCCESSFUL EXPANSION

continued to work hard on a machine as well as taking responsibility for the output of the production shop. The volume of mistakes and poor work has been steadily rising as sales have grown, but Fred has worked round the clock to sort them out before goods were released to customers. It has become clear that the firm's growth plans demand that the shop should now be professionally managed. After much heart-searching the owner has decided that Fred is not the man for the job. A person with management training and experience seems necessary to take the firm through its next stage of growth and beyond. Fred is therefore to be passed over very publicly, yet it is vital that his commitment to the firm's success is retained and that he does not in bitterness either walk out or work to undermine the new man.

Clearly it is not easy for the owner either to tell Fred of his decision or to keep his loyalty, but challenges like this really do face the owners of expanding firms. It need not arise in the production area nor with staff as transparently dedicated as Fred, but arise it almost certainly will.

The first general principle in meeting this situation must be honesty. If the owner owes Fred anything it is that. The second is objectivity, dealing with the facts of the firm's needs and the facts of recent performance under Fred's supervision. Keeping the discussion on this plane reduces the scope for emotional conflict. The third principle is patience. Fred may well speak bitterly, angrily and insultingly (and who can blame him?) but deep down he will probably be relieved. He knows he is not cut out for management and he feels he is letting the firm down through his substandard performance as a manager, yet can see no way of dealing with it, foreseeing a future in which the whole problem snowballs out of control. If this is in his mind he might not admit it, but could concentrate on the problem of loss of face before his workmates. It could take a long time to get to this stage, where the decision is accepted even if grudgingly, and the focus moves to its implementation. Someone with Fred's gifts and attitudes could be invaluable in the fields of quality control and research and development. Those, and other opportunities to put Fred to useful work in the firm, will present themselves by the time a full-time production manager has been engaged. Timing of this discussion is also important. It would be crass to hold it on Fred's wedding anniversary, for instance, or first thing on a Monday morning. Best of all would be to hold it on a Friday evening just after everyone has gone home, having first checked with Fred that he is not anxious to be away on time. Fred and his wife can then talk it over during the weekend, and such is the commonsense influence that most spouses exert that he will probably be able to talk soberly about it by Monday morning.

If the boss handles the interview badly Fred could become a bitter man whose health eventually breaks down under the corrosive effect of humiliation. Few bosses could live happily with that on their consciences, yet even fewer are prepared for the possibility of having to deal with such situations as a direct result of setting out on the growth path.

Systems and people

Employees expect the boss to want to know what is going on, and respect him for his concern to keep standards high. The systems used to keep management in the picture are explored in detail in Chapter 4. Here we shall look briefly at the way in which they affect the firm's people.

Knowing that one will have to report on one's performance and explain shortfalls is bracing. Knowing that exaggerations or lies will be detected quickly and will become a disciplinary matter encourages accuracy. Additionally, nobody will want his workmates to be aggrieved because he is responsible for making their jobs more difficult. To increase this sense of personal responsibility, all employees must be made aware of the interrelationship of all the separate jobs within the firm. Introducing control systems helps to do this, and allows people to see how important it is to complete all records fully to enable the systems, and hence the firm, to work properly. Thus a sound understanding among employees of a rational, simple control system can help the cohesiveness of the firm.

There is another sense in which the word 'control' is used in relation to people, to mean controlling their actions. Just as nations consent to be governed and will eventually overthrow any excessively oppressive regime, so employees give up to the boss their freedom of decision and action only in part and on condition that they are treated reasonably. They are perfectly free at any time to withdraw their labour, temporarily or permanently, if they feel that they are being ill-treated. Therefore, in the strict mechanical sense, their behaviour cannot be controlled as the speed of a car can. The horse consents to be ridden but reserves the right to baulk if asked to do too much.

SUCCESSFUL EXPANSION

It may withdraw consent altogether by throwing the rider if pressed too hard to do the unacceptable. Yet, handled properly by someone in whom it has confidence, it amplifies and extends greatly the powers of its rider. This analogy must not be pressed too far, but it carries a useful message.

Staff will push themselves if they can see the need and accept their responsibility to contribute extra effort. They have to feel it is really necessary, and it is part of management's leadership responsibility to inculcate that spirit by communicating clearly with the staff, and not forgetting to recognise it and thank them after the event. Coercion can have its place as a last resort but it is risky. The person whose extra effort is most needed may be given the hardest push, with the counter-productive result that he walks out. It is therefore to be used selectively and with caution.

The boss controlling his own activity

Most of us start off with more or less the same level of intelligence and expectation of time on earth, yet some achieve greatness and others fail to shine at anything, however modestly. The main distinguishing feature is the use people make of their time. Working long hours is not itself the answer. The high achiever uses time better, packing in more relevant and effective activity and effort through recognising where effort will be best rewarded and concentrating on that to the exclusion of most other things. If combined with excessively long hours this can lead to an inability to do anything but work, but if it is controlled it can be very powerful, at the same time enabling some sort of a normal life to be led.

The first task, therefore, is to recognise the activities that will be most rewarding. This search can be helped, in parallel, by looking for those that are known definitely to be unrewarding. Those in the first category the boss will ensure he has intimate knowledge of, day by day. Some he will keep for himself, but as growth forces him to delegate he will still have them automatically reported on to himself. Those in the second category need separating into activity which will be unrewarding, or a less rewarding way of spending time than the chosen alternative, and activity attracting painful penalties for non-performance. Anything that is in itself unrewarding, the absence of which punishes the firm severely, clearly needs to be done but rarely needs the personal attention of the chief executive. Best results under this heading are got by setting up proper systems at the outset. Thus imminent expiry of a vehicle's MOT certificate will automatically be notified by the system and someone at a low level in the organisation will deal with its renewal, without its ever being notified to the boss.

WORK PLANS
If the boss or his managers allow it, their days can be filled very busily with work that achieves little or nothing. To prevent this, minds must be cleared of trivia and enabled to concentrate on what matters. A useful device to encourage this is the work plan. This is a simple list in note form of jobs to be done this week, without fail. It does not matter what crops up unexpectedly and creates diversions, the boss commits himself to clearing the list each week. Asking the same of his managers and supervisors is to invite them to adopt a similarly useful discipline, and insisting that he has a copy of the work plans of his immediate subordinates at a fixed time every Friday afternoon, with a report on how well the plan for the previous week was fulfilled, can help managers to keep their concentration on the job in hand. They can also use the method on any subordinates who have some discretion over how time is spent. The boss has the moral right to require these things to be done only if he imposes the same discipline on himself.

There is scientific evidence to back up one's feeling that much activity is wasted. It will be explored in more detail in Chapter 4, but it is enough to say here that roughly one-fifth of what one does produces four-fifths of one's results. The real winners are the people who identify that highly significant minority of activities and concentrate on them.

CURBING IMPETUOSITY
Another aspect of the boss's control over himself is to curb his impetuousness, if possible without losing his entrepreneurial flair, so that he acts wisely at all times. It goes without saying that, however provoked, he should control his temper. Keeping cool is absolutely necessary to sound judgement and wise dealings. Decisions taken or actions performed in the heat of the moment are usually regretted long afterwards. Shouting at an employee demeans the dignity of the manager, and can also lead to unpleasant evidence at an industrial tribunal. Anyone who seeks to control anything or anyone else must always act judiciously, the first step towards which is to control himself.

SUCCESSFUL EXPANSION

Another aspect of impulsiveness is to take commercial decisions too fast. In the West many managers pride themselves on the speed of their decision-making. Decisiveness seems to confirm their toughness and other admirable frontier values. Procrastination and indecision have no place in the effective manager's tool-kit, but excessive speed can be equally deadly if it means that not enough evidence is assembled and too little time given to considering it. It is interesting here to contrast two different cultures of the West and Japan. Generally, the West admires the individualist who is quick on the draw, yet in Japan this is thought to be most irresponsible and eccentric. The Japanese will involve large numbers of personnel in a decision, all of whom will assemble information which will be painstakingly considered by everyone in the group. After this seemingly interminable process the decision will be taken and implemented very quickly indeed. By that time the western sharpshooter may be trying to climb out of the hole in which his impetuosity has landed him. One of the things the easterners do during their long meetings is to work out exactly how the decision will be implemented after it has been taken. Not only does that equip them to implement the decision with amazing speed, but also to foresee possible problems before they cause them, and thus to avoid them altogether.

PUBLIC BEHAVIOUR

Finally, to echo some points made previously, the boss must consider every aspect of his public behaviour if he is to gain and retain employees' respect and unstinting effort. He should always be available for contact during office hours, and never be inaccessible on the golf course. His behaviour to his staff should be equitable and impeccable. Before rewarding himself with a Ferrari he should think of the effect this will have on the staff, and perhaps settle for a luxury Ford. His dress sets an example of what is expected — truly every aspect of his presentation of himself influences staff attitudes and motivation in some way. And on a severely practical level, the owner of a car costing more than the average house would have some difficulty in persuading the staff that the company could not afford to pay them better. Even the nationality of his car is worth pondering. The writer once saw an extraordinary incongruity of the sort that can arise when people fail to think: a Mercedes-Benz sporting a sticker exhorting readers to buy British-grown food.

Chapter 3
Strategic Planning for Results

Designs for the future come in all shapes and sizes, from vague pipe-dreams to precisely stated plans for action. The more remote the future the less defined the business plan can be, for the environment in which we operate is so inconstant. That is sometimes used as an argument for dismissing planning altogether, but it is a false one. Without an aim one could wander off in any direction, so an aim is obviously desirable. Once defined, it automatically begs the question of how it is to be reached, which is to say that a plan for reaching it is called for. Thus planning is indispensable for anyone wishing to get somewhere, like the small business owner seeking to expand.

Any strategic plan has to start with a clear statement of the overall aim that it is designed to achieve. In preparing the plan, the aim may be modified in the light of knowledge and what is deemed possible, but it will still be the plan's guiding light. The aim needs to be stated as precisely as possible, with a time given for its achievement. The expected completion time will be influenced by all sorts of factors — how ambitious the plan is, the strength of actual and potential competition, the economic outlook, resources available, the slope of learning curves, the nature of the market concerned, and a whole host of others. Some of these factors can be determined in advance, some can be guessed at and others will be learned as time goes on or will prove to be practically unknowable. It might sound as if knowing where one wants to go is the easy part and that planning how to get there is a bit more difficult. That could be misleading. Most people, asked what they want from life, cannot give a coherent answer, and their replies are likely to be full of inconsistencies. Admittedly, mapping-out the journey to the target will not be simplicity itself but a lot of careful thought needs to be given to exactly what one's ambitions are before entering on the next stage.

There is a lot of work involved in creating ambitious yet realistic plans. People who are good at their jobs are usually hard workers and lucky. The luck implies further, often unacknowledged, work at eliminating losing chances and identifying winners. Luck is probably more often bought by effort than bestowed supernaturally.

Once the ultimate position towards which the firm seeks to grow has been defined, the rest of the planning process can take on a direction, falling in behind the main objective.

The plan also has a further important function in the early years of the expansion. At that time the business will be borrowing increasing amounts of money, largely on promises. Without the plan the lenders will be able to see little more than a hole into which their money is going, with little idea of whether or when they will get a return. Lenders are usually acute business people who will want to see some shape to the borrower's ideas, preferably in the form of a business plan of the type under discussion. They are capable of spotting inconsistencies, indeed they will be looking out for them, so the plan must be carefully prepared.

The act of writing the plan helps to eliminate large numbers of attractive possibilities, whittling them down to the (usually one) shortest route to the objective. It also throws up evidence that certain proposals are nonsense — like mismatching sales forecasts with production capacity, an easy mistake to make without the discipline of having to think about it, and many more of the same type. If the plan is recorded only in the owner's head and nowhere else, he will be a brave man who guarantees to avoid all such errors.

In preparing the strategic plan it will help to treat the business as if it is divided up into departments, even though formal divisions have not yet been established. Not only does this simplify the task of writing it, but it foreshadows what will probably be an inevitable development as the company grows.

Elements of the plan

The general idea of the plan is to provide:

- ☐ A statement of the overall objective and a date for reaching it
- ☐ A statement of the methods to be used to reach the objective
- ☐ A summary of resources available and those to be sought
- ☐ A detailed operating plan for a convenient period ahead
- ☐ Financial budgets.

THE OVERALL OBJECTIVE

Not only must this be considered wtith painstaking care but the wording used must be precise. Generalisations with meaning only to the writer should be avoided. 'To have a comfortable standard of living but not to work too hard', is not clear enough. 'To have a controlling interest in a countrywide bicycle-retailing multiple consisting of at least 50 stores in large centres of population by the year 2000' is more the kind of statement towards which some drive can be made.

This insistence on precision is not merely pedantic. It comes from recognising the twin primary functions of this statement, to act as the guiding light for the entire firm and to communicate to backers the management's clear view of its future.

It is not necessary to think the objective through to the bitter end before even picking up a pen to deal with ways and means. It would be unwise to try, for one useful feature of this approach to planning is that it rapidly becomes clear that one needs to go back and forth through the plan, making changes to ensure consistency between the parts. Because of this some people find it easiest to start somewhere other than at the beginning.

One obvious place to set out from is the factor that limits growth. In most cases this is in the marketing area: if only sufficient orders were available production could rise and finance could be obtained. In such a case it makes sense to write a marketing plan that achieves the desired volumes and profits before doing much else. If that task proves to be beyond the ingenuity of the firm and its advisers, it is probably right to question the realism of the target that is being set and perhaps to modify it.

Even though the overall objective may be subject to some moulding in the early stages of the plan's preparation, its influence is nonetheless very strong. Once arrived at, it is unlikely to change radically because of the careful way in which it was originally designed to express the one desire and ambition of the owner. The only circumstances in which it would be likely to change dramatically, or be discarded altogether, are if the process of planning threw up new information about undesirable or unavoidable commitments or directions essential to reaching the goal, or if some upheaval in the business environment made it no longer realistic. The human factor may come into play too, in that the idea can lose its attraction and grip on the imagination as the implications are more carefully explored. That seems to be a perfect justification for the approach advocated, for it helps to ensure that mistakes are made the cheap way, on paper rather than in real life.

THE METHOD

This element in the planning process defines the company's proposed actions intended to reach the objective. While many owners of firms have got where they are partly because of their drive to get things done quickly and efficiently, it may be wise to restrain any tendency to do the whole thing oneself. If people are employed who are actual or potential heads of departments they could usefully be brought into the planning process by being asked to draw up the expansion plan in relation to their individual areas of responsibility. This should do a number of desirable things:

> Stop the boss making assumptions based on out-of-date knowledge of detail
> Get the benefit of the current experience of the person at the sharp end of the task
> Give the departmental head a sense of potential in his job
> Provide the boss with a measure of his subordinate's suitability for further responsibility.

To contribute to the full extent of their abilities, department heads will need a clearly defined guideline to work to, preferably the statement of the overall objective plus a summary of the rough outline for the next five years, arrived at during a meeting of the affected managers and the owner. If the owner cannot bring himself to disclose his plans sufficiently to let his key people in on the secret, he should at least provide enough precise, concrete information, in the way of targets perhaps, to make sure that they spend time trying to answer the question rather than fathoming exactly what the old man really means. There can be good reasons for withholding full information from managers about the firm's plans, but there will be a price for doing so. In such circumstances the managers cannot be blamed if they come up with less satisfactory plans than the owner feels he has a right to expect. If full information is not provided it should be made clear and a reason given. It should be emphasised that if this causes problems the owner is accessible to give guidance to managers who might otherwise soldier manfully on down a blind alley.

In this, as in other cases, the owner should examine his

motives for not fully informing his managers of his plans. They are the people who have to put plans into practice, after all, and can be expected to give more energy to carrying out ideas of their own, or ones they have influenced, than to ideas imposed on them from above. If at bottom the owner's real and only motive for keeping information secret is to boost his own importance, he will deserve and get inferior performance from his employees, and his firm will be poorer than it might have been.

The first stage of working out methods should intentionally be kept short. A couple of days should be enough for most people to have assembled their ideas on ways and means in a general and outline form. They could then meet to compare their views and reach a consensus acceptable to the owner. In most situations they would then go on to discuss the sales revenues and volumes sought, the channels and products to be involved, and the consequent expectations of cost and margins. Attention would then turn to production. To achieve output at the quantities and costs sought, particular investments may be needed. All of that can then be pulled together into a financial plan detailing working capital requirements, capital expenditure budgets, profit and loss budgets, cash flow forecasts and funding plans.

This is necessarily a simplified version of what happens. In real life there is much interplay between departments about what is possible and what is not. Sales people will probably want production colleagues to be infinitely flexible and impossibly cheap. Production and finance will want sales to sell what is easiest and most profitable to make, with as few variations as possible. Handled badly, the meeting could cause much rancour, but handled well by that wise chairman, the owner, the meeting will be constructive and will help managers to see the problems of the company as a whole as their joint problems.

The simplification is misleading in one further respect, namely the way in which the financial function is portrayed, merely as reacting to information fed to it by the operating divisions. Any financial specialist worth his salt will play a full part in helping managers to estimate and allocate overhead and other costs, thus ensuring that their schemes are not built on false accounting assumptions. It also helps the finance department to receive information that is of real use and censored of any proposals that have unattractive profitability. The finance man does not have a veto — that belongs to the boss — but he helps fellow-managers to understand the full financial implications of their ideas. They, in turn, will educate the finance man to see that in real life things are not always as predictable and perfect as an administrator would wish them to be, and that making things or providing services is the start of the whole commercial process. Without that operating activity there can be no costing system, no financial forecasts and budgets, and no management reports. In other words, the planning process might encourage them to start acting as a team rather than as warring individuals. It is natural and right for any manager to want to defend his department from the attacks of others, but the owner cannot afford to allow that to degenerate into the situation where time and effort are channelled into gathering evidence about the shortcomings of others in order to be able to hit back. If managers begin to behave negatively and defensively only the owner can sort it out.

At an early stage it therefore becomes possible to develop a sense of the importance of the plan and to use it to unify the approach of different parts of the company. To help this process the owner might consider naming the meetings held to monitor progress the strategy committee.

RESOURCES

Few ambitious expansions can be undertaken without access to extra resources from outside the company, although the odd example of growth funded entirely from the company's own cash flow is met from time to time. Typically, this is how some retailing expansions have been undertaken, especially in fast-moving goods. One grocery chain at least is said to have opened a new store every month or so without affecting its cash position. New stores were stocked up with goods on 30-day credit, but the goods were all sold for cash within the 30 days. The shopfitters were paid some months later when profits were coming through in cash. Thus the firm concerned had to meet only a modest wage bill for a few days before the money started to roll in. It was, of course, not quite as simple as that but this brief description captures the essence of the operation.

Most firms will not be so well placed, needing more or better machines and equipment, extra staff, or even completely new premises. Since it would be wasteful to bring in new resources until present ones are fully stretched, a useful starting-point for this part of the plan might be a thorough inventory of present resources, and how they might be made more productive at least cost.

To some extent that may be undertaken by an internal review, but often the clear gaze of an outsider is called for to challenge the assumptions inherent in existing practices. More on the subject of outside advisers appears in Chapter 5. There is a good deal of free or subsidised help available from competent specialists which it would be foolish to ignore.

Although examples from the realm of production have been used a lot so far, all the operational activities of the small business — administration, accounting, selling and so on as well — should come under the spotlight. As with so many things that ought to be done, the manner of doing it is important. The operating manager, department head or whatever his position may be, should not be given reason to feel that he is being checked on by the adviser for the purposes of a secret report to the boss. The manager will not be such a fool as to think that the adviser will form no opinion of his ability and suitability for the job, nor that his views will not reach the owner's ears. He should, however, be encouraged to see that as incidental to the main purpose of the visit, which is to help the firm and its employees to do their work better. It would probably be going too far the other way to assign the consultant entirely to the department manager, but sensitivity to the reactions of people is needed if the consultant is to be of maximum use to the firm.

The inventory thus compiled of the firm's resources and their capacities gives a useful indicator to how more efficient and more intensive use of present assets will improve profits and enable the early steps of the expansion to be put into effect. It also identifies the bottle-necks that must be removed, or the inhibiting factors to be overcome, for expansion to proceed beyond present capacity. The kind of inventory described rarely shows all resources in equilibrium. Either more can be made than sold, more can be painted than assembled, or more work could be taken on if working capital were sufficient, and so forth.

From there it is but a small step to specifying what options exist to expand output. Taking the instance of a bottle-neck in the assembly shop the range of choices might emerge as:

— Put assembly on to two-shift working
— Get a bigger factory
— Contract out some assembly

SUCCESSFUL EXPANSION

— Contract out another activity and expand assembly in the space vacated
— Change design or specifications to simplify assembly
— Change specification to eliminate painting and expand assembly in the spare space
— Take in contract painting work to fill the spare capacity, and so on.

Some of the options could be immediately rejected as being inconsistent with other imperatives. For instance, it might be felt that all assembly must be done in-house to control quality. There are still several realistic possibilities on that list which could overcome the problem, if only temporarily. Some might be inappropriate at the present time but become real possibilities later. Others might also add to earning power over and above any action taken on the assembly question — for example, filling spare capacity with contract work. Thus other opportunities emerge from the process of critically examining capacity, as well as the solution to frustrating bottle-necks.

OPERATING PLANS
Each department head, or the owner, if the firm has not yet reached the stage of employing them, will contribute a plan for each department to build up into the overall plan for the company as a whole. In addition a further useful purpose is served. Having to write down what they plan to achieve is a discipline on managers to think hard before they commit the company to expenditure, and before they rashly forecast impossible levels of performance. It is particularly useful in discouraging any tendency to tell the boss what they think he wants to hear, rather than their sober assessment of the facts. It extends the principle, already stated, of encouraging them to see the company as a whole and to check with other departments how their plans impinge on one another. There is little point in the production manager saying in isolation that he will make 50,000 widgets when the sales manager plans to sell 10,000. (Widgets, for anyone unfamiliar with them, is a made-up name for imaginary products.) The managers should have resolved inconsistencies by the time they write down their plans, with the owner on hand to act as referee and give encouragement to the faint-hearted when necessary.

Year 1 should be specified in some detail with subsequent years' intentions given in outline. Each department should show its plans in the form of budget appropriate to it, that is to say in figures, with whatever supporting narrative or notes may be necessary.

FINANCIAL BUDGETS

Once the operating plans are available, agreed between managers, and approved by the owner, they can be turned into financial budgets. Year 1 will be shown in full, and profit and loss figures and cash flow forecasts broken down monthly. Managers then use them as their minimum standards of acceptable performance. The owner can monitor them too to alert him when any department or budget item is straying from plan.

The financial function will have assessed day-to-day working capital needs, or at least month to month, from the operating plans and budget, and negotiated accordingly with the bank to cover any temporary cash shortfall. The bank will have assigned to its customer an overdraft limit beyond which it will not pay cheques drawn on the account. If the overdraft is to be exceeded the owner needs to be the first to know, and certainly will wish to tell the bank before the event. Much of the basis on which banks lend to firms is their assessment of the managements involved. Quite reasonably, they form a poor judgement of a firm that forecasts one performance yet delivers another, especially if the owner does not know why. Provided the initiative comes from him, there is nothing wrong in the owner returning to the bank with up-to-date information on how the position arose, and corrective action planned and taken, with clear, plausible explanations of why he will need to have the overdraft limit raised. It is always preferable to tell the bank what is happening rather than leave them to find out.

As any student of accounting knows, working capital requirements can increase if sales are below forecast, just as easily as if they are above. The owner's constant vigilance over results compared with budget will enable him to ensure that action is taken quickly to put the firm's house in order financially.

As for more distant needs, work can start on refining the estimated figures given for future years. In fairly short order, next year's outline plan needs to be turned into a detailed forecast and budget, and early warning of the financial implications is helpful.

SUCCESSFUL EXPANSION

Putting the plan together

The great questions of 'Who, what, why, when, where, how?' having been answered, the plan can now be pulled together. A key aspect which the owner will have been balancing throughout the planning process is the need, on one hand, to keep the plan flexible to allow for updating and correction as time goes on, and on the other hand to make commitments to particular courses of action, some of which are irrevocable. As individual circumstances vary so much, no general rule is serviceable, except perhaps that cautious companies seem to have a tendency to survive. They do not avoid risk altogether, but seek to minimise it and take only considered decisions. Not for them the irresistible bargain that must be bought today or not at all.

This chapter emphasises planning for results. Clearly, no results will emerge if the plan now disappears into a drawer and is forgotten, labelled as yet another of the old man's whims. If it is to serve its true purpose it must be used to stimulate action directed towards its aim, the attainment of the company's overall objective. How this can come about is covered in the next chapter.

Chapter 4
Keeping on Course

In an ideal world it would be easy to portray two types of firm. Everything that could go wrong in one of them would, and writers of books like this could glibly point out that the firm was controlling the management, not the other way round. In the other type of firm, by contrast, each manager would have perfect foresight, enabling him to avoid problems and all staff would get clear instructions which they would follow to the letter. Here, the reader would be invited to conclude, management is in the saddle and means to stay there.

Real life is rarely as pat as that. As things are, it obviously makes sense to strive to be closer to the latter example than the former. A realist, however, will recognise that problems will arise and can probably congratulate himself if most of the problems that do occur crop up in areas beyond the direct control of the firm and its managers. To demand more of himself and his managers is essential, or how would improvements ever come about, but to *expect* more would lead to disappointment.

Management control

The management that has its operations under little control is likely to spend much time on fire-fighting — producing short-term answers to pressing problems of the moment. Firemen put fires out quickly and effectively, but the damage from the water is often greater than that from the fire. Commercially, the same lesson applies: the solution to one difficulty produces other problems which must be dealt with in turn. This is largely due to the haste with which fire-fighting solutions have to be found. Everyone knows that solutions themselves cause further problems, but in emergencies the knock-on effects have to be accepted, and dealt with in due course. Once a management has got itself into the fire-fighting mode of operation, the odds are that it will be locked into it.

SUCCESSFUL EXPANSION

The first step towards avoiding that deadly situation is careful planning of future action, taking trouble to foresee the inevitable problems arising from actions, and allowing for them before they happen. The second step, the subject of this chapter, is the development of a system to control the firm's course, keeping it as close as possible to the one that was planned, while at the same time giving sufficiently early notice of revisions that may need to be made to the plan.

For a control system to work there must be:

- ☐ Clear demarcation of individual responsibilities throughout the firm
- ☐ Clearly-defined targets, preferably numerical, agreed as achievable by those responsible for meeting them
- ☐ Availability of information in appropriate form, of adequate accuracy and sufficiently quickly, to enable judgements to be made of performance against targets
- ☐ A mechanism for communicating and implementing, in a timely manner, decisions arising from comparison of actual performance with target.

A paperwork fanatic could probably take those statements and apply them to provide work for four administrators in a one-man firm. A commonsense approach is needed, for there is a double cost attached to gathering information: it takes people's time, which costs money, and stops them from doing something productive, which loses the chance to make money.

Simplicity is therefore important, but so is sensitivity – the system must cause a reaction when something goes wrong. It might not tell management the cause, but if it barks loudly enough to stimulate further probing, it will have served its purpose. The manager needs to act when things go wrong (or preferably beforehand), not when they are all right.

A company's normal profit and loss accounts, rendered monthly, are a useful tool for the owner, for he needs to see the whole picture. They will be of little help to the heads of departments in terms of control over their own activity. Thus, different records need to be kept which are not those of the conventional historical accounting process, but belong to the field of management accounting.

Management accounting

Management accounting deals with the figures needed for

actually running the business, and therefore looks into the future. This is very different from the activity normally associated with the accounts function: retrospective reporting of what happened. The management accountant deals with such matters as costing and liquidity control, things of the present and immediate future. The conventional accountant deals with the past and must work in precise figures to satisfy statutory requirements. In management accounting reports, absolute precision is rarely called for. It takes so long to achieve that the information may have aged to the point of uselessness by the time it is available. One management accounting concept which the owner will need to grapple with is the trade-off between precision and timeliness. He can have exact figures in two months' time, or very inexact figures half an hour after the end of the week. He may well settle for something in between — circumstances and needs vary from firm to firm — but the point is that the information system is there to serve him, not the other way round. Each firm is therefore free to set up a system that suits it.

While the function of management accounting is different from that of historical accounting, the information it generates is closely related to the normal accounting conventions. The whole idea is to keep a grip on events in order to ensure that they produce results as close as possible to the financial plan. That plan, it will be recalled, is presented in conventional accounting terms. As the firm grows it might decide to invest in some computer power to strengthen its grasp on what is happening. Indeed, it will not have to grow very much before it becomes affordable. When that point is reached it will be able to produce, with little effort, not only its own management control reports, but also full sets of accounts every week or every month. This is the computer fulfilling its true purpose of reducing human drudgery and making more information available, so that people can take more informed decisions and be more in control of complex events.

The example on page 54 shows a simple budget for a straightforward one-man manufacturing and repair firm. Let us say he is a blacksmith. In order to get his target income and cover his overheads, which are easy to predict, he has to sell 1200 hours of time at £11.60 per hour. Thus his control over profitability is weekly, or even daily. If he fails to sell 25 hours' work a week, or gets less than £11.60 per hour, or does so for less than 48 weeks a year, he knows he will miss his year's target. At the end of each week all he has to do to check up is to add up that week's labour charges on invoices and work in progress; if it comes to at least £290 (£11.60 x 25) he knows he is home and dry and can have a happy weekend. If it is less, he needs to find out why and take corrective action. That, in essence, is what the control system is about — finding the key calculation which determines performance, keeping informed about it in as uncomplicated a way as possible, and acting when things go wrong. The example contrasts with the way so many one-man, and larger, firms are run, in which nobody knows whether a year was profitable until the books come back from the accountant, perhaps six months after the year-end. Such firms are obviously out of control.

		£	
Budget	Sales	20,000	*Control*
	Materials	6,000	1,200 chargeable hours
	Value added	14,000	@ £11.60 — weekly target 25 hours of chargeable work for 48 weeks per year.
	Overheads and Drawings	14,000	

In the larger firm, and particularly one with ambitions to expand, rather more sophisticated controls need to be applied. Nonetheless, the sense must be preserved of the need to deal only with essentials. There is a temptation to elaborate controls to the point where they explain everything. This is wasteful of time which should be better spent on making profits. The essentials common to every firm are liquidity, costs, production and invoiced sales. In some firms, especially manufacturers, forward orders are important and can be added to the list. The efficiency of the firm in getting goods out through the door and invoiced, and payments collected, can all emerge from a little detailing of the essentials listed above. Even with those refinements the list is still short and should be manageable.

Within individual departments the owner will reasonably expect control to be kept over important matters affecting their performance. Over a period, informal systems of considerable merit may have been developed. It would be foolish and insensitive to throw these systems out if they, or something very similar, could be built into the overall control system. If a computer is used the complexity involved will pose few problems. An example might be in the production area. Quantity of output will obviously be measured, but records should also be kept of quality failures and their source. Without them the cause cannot be accurately placed under its right heading from a list which would include human failing, substandard materials, poor design, unsatisfactory machinery or substandard bought-in components. If the cause is wrongly diagnosed, much energy will be spent in introducing inappropriate solutions, while the problem rumbles on, possibly gathering momentum and becoming more difficult to solve.

For the control system to work, everyone associated with it must understand its importance. While the owner may be used to dealing with figures and appreciate their significance and purpose, many of his staff may see them as meaningless chores inflicted on them for no good reason, and others as an instrument of persecution. It does not take much temptation for someone with those attitudes to put down invented figures, just to fill in the spaces, or to try getting away with not completing their returns at all. As a general rule, not only should people be told how important it is, but they should also be required to present their figures as a report on their performance, with explanations of any deviations from target. That helps them to concentrate on the essentials represented by the target, and to see that performance reports have a great practical value to the firm. This approach need not be confined to managers, as a machine operator can easily explain why output was less than his budget, as well as reporting the bare figures of what was produced. A further benefit is that the raw data are turned into information at each stage of reporting and information is what gets people thinking. An example of this principle is the comparison between a book of cheque stubs and paying-in slips, and a bank statement. Both contain the same data, but the bank statement processes the data into information on the progress of the account and its latest position.

What needs to be controlled?

In any jungle the first necessity is to stay alive: the commercial jungle is no exception. Once immediate threats to existence have been overcome or avoided, longer-term survival can be addressed. Only then is it worth looking at improving the quality of life.

Once the firm is established, the factors necessary to short-term economic survival are:

—|Liquidity: the ability to pay bills

— Protection from catastrophe: sudden disablement of the owner, fire, flood, severe breach of the law etc.

In the longer term more is required than appears on that brief list. Short term, however, it is of paramount importance to control the item which can be controlled — liquidity — and to obtain cover, probably by a combination of insurance and prudence, against the second eventuality.

Liquidity is itself improved in the short term by:

- ☐ Receiving payments from customers
- ☐ Not paying suppliers
- ☐ Investment in, and loans to, the firm: in the short term this usually means raising the level of overdraft
- ☐ Retained profits.

The last item on this list is influenced by longer-term considerations although its absence can have a rapid, short-term effect. It is within the power of the owner to exercise day-to-day control over the first three items. In most small firms they should be reviewed at least once a week and positive, vigorous action taken where appropriate.

The small firm usually obtains most of its purchases from larger suppliers to whom it is an insignificant customer. The ability to delay payment is severely limited unless the firm is to take unacceptable risks over having supplies cut off. The overdraft limit has usually been fixed and may be rather inflexible at short notice, though given time and a number of favourable factors it may be possible to negotiate an increase. Thus the aspects of a small firm's liquidity most susceptible to management action are the speed with which it issues invoices after completing orders, and the chasing of customers for payment. Even here there may be constraints, and there almost certainly will be.

Some very large companies have a stated policy of withholding payment for 90 days, which makes them impervious to cajoling or even threats from a small supplier. Other firms have no stated policy, but simply try to trade as much as possible on suppliers' money. They probably keep waiting for a month or two those whom they need most, and those from whom they are unlikely to buy again they do not pay until the writ arrives, or at least the threat of one. Finally, there are a blessed few who pay quickly. There is no point in adding an extra delay by failing to invoice as soon as work is done, a point often overlooked.

The great excuse used by the 'keep 'em waiting' school of customers is that the payment is stuck in the computer. Yet, curiously, they have no difficulty in paying promptly powerful creditors who refuse to wait: the tax authorities, Customs and Excise, road tax, court fines; none offers generous credit and some demand instant settlement. The computer manages to pay them, but not the small supplier. The truth is, of course, that the speed with which suppliers are paid is a management decision, and management decisions can be influenced. The main pressure the small firm can bring to bear relates to how the deal was set up in the first place; if the customer specifically agreed to pay inside seven days, the supplier could institute collection procedures much sooner than if he agreed 30 days or, worse still, if it was not discussed at all.

Companies dealing directly with the public, or selling small items or services to business, are often better placed to collect cash on delivery. Not all of them take most people's fair-mindedness into account when settling payment terms. Firms who have sold to business often assume that a customer expects the goods first, then an invoice. If they begin to sell to the public they can greatly improve cash flow by asking for a deposit in advance and the balance on delivery. Members of the public expect to buy like that. If the product is being made to special order — say a fitted kitchen, the deposit can quite reasonably be very substantial, up to 50 per cent being paid before fitting. One small kitchen manufacturer has a clause in his contract reserving title to the goods he sells. This means that they remain his property until paid for. He takes a 25 per cent deposit with order, a further 50 per cent on delivery of the units to the customer's house (totalling 75 per cent before he actually installs anything) and the balance of 25 per cent a month after fitting. This means that the cost of materials bought and work done are covered before he does anything irrevocable by way of fixing things to walls. Once fitted, the units cannot legally be snatched back, even if they are not paid for. Equally, his customer retains a sizeable sum against any errors in making or fitting, and, above all, his liquidity is high because he often gets paid before he has to pay his timber supplier.

Customers who have not paid should be chased promptly and firmly. The company which makes quick payment a condition of sale gives itself a head start. Chasing slow payers is better done by personal contact or telephone. If it must be by letter, it

SUCCESSFUL EXPANSION

should be addressed personally to a named individual. The standard photocopied letter to a firm, the sticker — sometimes jokey — on statements, the rubber-stamped message on a statement: all of these are so common now as to be devalued and ineffective. It is much harder to ignore a personal approach.

For overdue invoices to be chased it is necessary for them to be identified in the first place. To this end, the owner will probably want to install the control of an aged debtors' list. This will be a report of which a shortened form is:

Aged debtors' list at 27 March 1984

			\multicolumn{4}{c}{Overdue}			
Customer	Total £	Current £	1 month £	2 months £	3 months £	Over 3 months £
Arnold	1,452	1,085	250	103	–	14
Eliot	4,953	–	–	–	961	3,992
Dickens	143	75	68	–	–	–
Total	6,548	1,160	318	103	961	4,006
Percentage	100	18	5	2	14	61

The overall position is appalling. Three-fifths of all the money owed to the firm is more than three months overdue and is nearly all down to one customer, Eliot. He (or she) has not bought from the firm for three months, which suggests that a different supplier is being used, or production has been run down considerably. The firm may find it more difficult to get paid than if Eliot had remained a customer, and might not get paid at all if that firm is going broke. Since three-quarters of the debts are owed by Eliot, the implications are very serious indeed. The owner, having neglected his job so far, should get down to Eliot's straight away and camp out on the doorstep until he gets paid.

Dickens, on the other hand, does not need the personal attention of the owner. He is a small, regular customer who needs only a letter or phone call to get a cheque for £68 in the post. Arnold has bought a much larger consignment in the current month than before. While that does not need chasing now, a careful eye will be kept on his payment record. It might have been wiser to ask him to split his order into two or three parts, each of which would be invoiced and paid for before the next was delivered. As it is, no further orders will be processed until he has paid for the current month's delivery, even if they arrive before the debt becomes overdue. Someone needs to chase the outstanding payments, the oldest of which is probably some adjustment for discount or damaged goods. Needless to say, this should all have been done before Arnold placed the current large order.

So much for the points to watch for to ensure that the firm survives from day to day. That is obviously not the whole story, as there are longer-term forces at work too. The main ones needing regular, close attention are:

- ☐ Profitability
- ☐ Order book
- ☐ Customer service
- ☐ Supplier service
- ☐ Competitive performance.

The firm will have budgeted to sell a certain volume of its products at particular prices, in specified quantities and at defined costs, to arrive at the budgeted level of profitability. In building up those assumptions it will have made further assumptions, such as the mix of orders from customers buying on different discounts, raw materials prices, the cost of transport, and so on. In an ideal situation, information on all of these will be instantly available. Microcomputers make that possible, but under a paperwork system it may prove too time-consuming for the value of the information most of the time, although special situations will exist in some businesses which demand up-to-date knowledge. In the competitive world of mass-market jewellery manufacturing, for instance, a company can have the highest possible productive efficiency and still sink without trace if it once buys its gold and silver at the wrong prices. The critical factors there, the fluctuations in the precious metals futures markets, are far more influential than production efficiencies in determining the product's ex-works price. Finding the critical factor and watching it daily, or even more often, is crucial in any business where the cost of the product is dominated by that one factor. Where it is a combination of a small number of factors, this same principle applies. Where the cost structure is less lopsided, the task is no easier — everything has to be closely controlled. It can be a useful exercise occasionally to analyse the profitability of groups of products, or of groups of customers or industries to which the firm sells. If it shows that there are passengers, action can be taken.

Many businesses measure their anxiety or confidence about the future in terms of their order book. If it is full for a healthy period ahead, work can be planned, materials ordered, and perhaps extra staff taken on. If the order book stretches too far into the future, thoughts will turn to possible loss of disappointed customers and opportunities for expansion. Often, expansions take place under such circumstances for largely defensive reasons: to discourage new competitors from coming into existence and existing competitors from themselves expanding. Thus the proprietor of the firm will wish to keep a close check on the state of the order book, product by product, as well as in total. The check on individual products is especially important because salesmen will always be tempted to sell only the popular products, and neglect the rest. They may try to convince the owner that there is no need to sell the less popular products in busy times, as they are reaching their sterling sales targets without them. They may say in lean times that the unpopular products are impossible to sell. The company's interest lies in the other direction: less popular products can be sold on the back of successful ones in good times as well as bad, and the company needs every profitable sale it can get, at any time.

The order book should also break down the sales of each product to different customer groups. Thus early warning will be given of a tendency for one or two large, high-discount customers to dominate buying, with a resulting fall in profitability. Early corrective action can be taken to stimulate sales to low-discount outlets, which lowers the average discount taken overall.

If there are to be enough orders, or even any at all, the owner needs to keep close control over customer service. This consists of matters that can be measured, as well as those which are difficult or impossible to measure, springing as they do from attitudes of mind. Measurable items include speed of response to sales enquiries, delays in answering calls for service engineers, delivery times, damage to goods in transit, and the like. Once again, the important ones in a particular firm need to be identified and then reported on routinely. As ever, the report not only states the facts and explains deviations from the agreed norm, but also says what is being done to correct any problems. Most firms would probably not require this report more often than monthly.

Aspects of service that cannot be measured are, naturally, more difficult to track, yet they may be the most important in the long run. They include the way that the telephone is answered, how letters are written, the whole projection of the company's image from letterhead design through cleanliness of vehicles to the salesmen's clothing and the way that they speak to customers. The formally designed communications, like letterhead and publicity, will largely be under the owner's control, and he can easily check on the condition of any of his vehicles that call at the company's base. He can cause telephone calls to be made to see how long the phone rings and how helpfully and politely the caller is dealt with. He can check on the quality of typing and English in the letters written on behalf of the firm. In the early days he will probably be the only person writing them, but with expansion he needs to check just occasionally to see that others are keeping up his standards. He can accompany salesmen on their rounds from time to time, to see how they are received by customers and how they behave (this is also a good motivator for the salesmen, who will be keen to make an impression on the boss; and on the customer, who is flattered to be visited by the top man and will relish the chance to explain his company's shortcomings to his face. Such visits can be eye-openers).

Because he cannot read and correct every letter, nor be present at every sales visit, nor monitor every telephone conversation, the owner has either to trust his staff to perform properly, or construct mechanisms for monitoring output. His confidence in their performance can be greatly improved if each department has a reliable method of evaluating output against company norms, and continuous training can keep it up to scratch. People do so easily slip into ways of working that are not necessarily the best, and constant vigilance by top management is the only way of securing reasonable certainty that things are being done properly.

Just as the customer will want good service, so the supplier has a right to seek a profit from supplying him. From time to time, perhaps annually, it could be useful to evaluate one's customers at both ends of the spectrum. The very large may well buy at rock-bottom prices, as well as demanding extra services and wanting everything done yesterday. To cap it all, they will probably take an age to pay bills. A profit and loss account for big customers may show a loss. Equally, it may be concluded that the loss involved in serving them is more than offset by the extra volume that their custom brings. Such an analysis is especially necessary when the supplier is thinking of expanding production, and possibly even moving to bigger premises. Careful analysis and a lot of thought may show that he needs not a bigger factory but one customer less, in consequence of which he will work less hard and make more profit. Or, put another way, the terms given to that customer need radical revision if he is to be worth keeping.

The smallest customers can be unprofitable to deal with if they are given the full range of services. Hence the proliferation at trade counters of notices saying 'Minimum order for trade discount £50', or 'Minimum order on credit accounts £20, all others cash', and 'Delivery free up to 10 miles on orders over £100'. All of them are designed to reduce the fixed cost per order of running credit accounts or a delivery service, or of simply having warehouse staff scurrying about for small customers while larger ones wait. The levels at which the thresholds are set for the full service are, or should be, based on analysis, rather than plucking figures out of the air. The manager will take into account the costs of serving smaller customers and set off against them a calculation of the sales, and hence the margin, likely to be lost if such conditions are imposed.

For there to be goods to sell to customers, the owner needs suppliers. He will have to walk a difficult path between extracting promises of service from them and holding them to their undertakings on one hand, and on the other cultivating the relationship so that he is given preferential treatment when supplies are short or when some bargain lot becomes available to be offered to 'good' customers. As he relinquishes direct involvement with buying he will want to ensure that his subordinates do not become over-eager to secure the best deal at the expense of a valuable, almost personal, relationship. This might involve walking another difficult path set by the need to determine how the supplier sees his firm as a customer, while not wishing to appear to his staff as if he is going behind their backs.

Competitors' activities need monitoring for obvious reasons. Unfortunately, the people closest to them, the sales force, can be prone to assume that what is obvious to them is common knowledge. Sales personnel should therefore be encouraged to send in competitors' leaflets, price-lists, and other material that may be freely available, as well as reporting on documents giving quotations and offering special terms to particular customers.

The whole point of a control system is to attract attention to deviations from plan, so that appropriate corrective action can be instituted. Decisions need to be taken rapidly as the need for them becomes apparent, because one of the advantages that the small firm has over its larger competitors is its speed of response and ability to adapt quickly to changing situations. To delay would be to remove a major advantage and to behave, in effect, like an under-sized big firm: plodding and slow to adapt, but lacking the momentum of size and the large firm's bigger firepower. Sometimes this implies taking unpopular and unpleasant decisions gravely affecting other people's lives. Nevertheless, the survival of the firm is the paramount consideration and the logic of the information must be followed, ruthlessly if need be.

A word on computers. Absolutely the wrong way to select one is to attend dealers' demonstrations and come away bemused and impressed by the power of their machines. It is better to specify the performance that is required of the system, and to put that specification out for quotes to the dealers for the various makes. In that way the buyer is more likely to concentrate on essentials and to stay in command, and less likely to be dazzled by the optional extras. Another benefit of this method of buying is that the machine and its programs are bought from one source. If they are bought separately, the software man can blame the machine for any problems, and the hardware man can blame the programs. The act of thinking about the requirements of the system sometimes helps owners to see that they do not need a computer at all (for the time being at least), but to clean up their manual systems. Absolutely the wrong reason to buy a computer is in the hope that it will sort out a chaotic manual system. It will not, for the computer needs a clear, logical system to be able to make any contribution at all. The right course of action is, therefore, to organise a really effective manual system, and to look on the computer as merely a possible aid to faster calculation and greater sophistication in the presentation of information.

Although the electronics of computers are virtually everlasting, the mechanical parts are not yet as reliable. Consequently, an important part of the task of evaluating a supplier and his systems is the availability of quick, effective service. A first-rate system with poor back-up is worse than an also-ran with a good, local, service facility. Similarly, the stability of the dealer needs to be taken into account: will he be in existence in a few years' time when service is likely to be most needed?

Tax authorities like to be sure that computerised systems are sound. Therefore, the company's accountant must be involved in the decision.

Chapter 5
Advice and Advisers

People who start businesses must have confidence in their own ability. That confidence is an essential working tool and it would be quite wrong for them to do anything that undermines it. Self-confidence carried to excess can be a weakness, however, especially if it leads to the view that there is nothing to learn from others. The man who listens to other people's ideas may conclude that, on the topic under discussion, he has gained little or nothing. He may see that far from seeking to advise him, the person he is listening to is trying to sell him something. Or he may conclude that the other man is a fool.

None of these objections invalidates the wisdom of using other people's advice continuously. Note the word 'using' — the idea of taking advice is different from that of using it. Taking advice is not the idea behind listening to people's views. One may end up doing something identical, or remarkably close, to what someone suggested, but that will often be after a lot of mental processing of that idea, and others, before any decision is reached.

The idea behind the notion of using advice is to cast one's net widely before taking a decision, on the assumptions that:

— Nobody has a monopoly of knowledge: valuable facts can be cited by the most unlikely people.
— Nobody has a monopoly of wisdom: other people can suggest original ways of getting to the objective that have not occurred to oneself.
— Listening to a sequence of conventional solutions can strengthen one's conviction that a radical approach is needed and can work.
— People who are at home in a territory unknown to oneself can save much time otherwise spent expensively learning elementary rules.
— Learning about the snags in one's ideas helps to improve them.

— Very occasionally, a completely new perspective on a problem is revealed in discussion, which leads to a once-in-a-lifetime breakthrough.

The businessman has sole responsibility for his actions and cannot pass it on to advisers. If he takes advice, that is, he uncritically follows the suggestion of another, and things go wrong, he may feel aggrieved and blame the adviser, which flies in the face of the principle of his responsibility for his own decisions. Since the whole idea is to win the battle, it is rather pointless to lose but have a scapegoat handy.

If advisers are used, rather than obeyed, they can (to continue the military analogy) illuminate areas that were only dimly seen, and often highlight massive forces that were previously completely invisible. But responsibility for understanding what is seen, and how it affects the owner's plans, still rests with him alone. Thus, if advisers are to be used well, they will be taken into the firm's confidence and encouraged to explain how they see the scene and the proposals, or else they cannot operate helpfully. After sifting all the advice he has received, and putting together that which he has not rejected, the owner will be in a position to take a better-informed decision.

When deciding what advice to accept or reject, two temptations should be avoided. Life seems easier if inconvenient truths are overlooked, but it will certainly become more difficult later on, and more expensive, for the business person who does so. It is far better to welcome the new facts on board and redesign the approach to take them into account, if it is indeed necessary to do so. It will be uncomfortable at first, but the policy will be more relevant and the stronger for it in the end. The other temptation is to be swayed by persuasive or dogmatic statements of opinion. The opinions of others are worth seeking and considering, but the main concern must be the facts that led to the forming of those opinions. As everyone knows, people given the same set of facts or objectives can come to diametrically opposed views on what action is proper.

The loyalties of advisers can run in a number of different directions. A chartered accountant's loyalty, for instance, is primarily to his professional standards of behaviour, and only after that to his client. That may be inconvenient for the businessman who wants professional blessing for unethical actions, but it does have the great advantage that the accountant's word on his client's behalf is usually trusted by the authorities, and that his advice will be directed towards the interests of the client, rather than the misuse of professional confidence to fleece him. On the other hand, someone trying to sell something will have his advice received in the light of his obvious self-interest. That does not invalidate his advice, the main use of which will be the underlying facts that he presents, some of which may come as quite a surprise. The very fact that he stands to gain forces him to support his arguments with information that can be independently shown to be true, some of which might well be uncomfortable truths which the owner needs to know.

Banks

Somewhere in the middle fall the banks. Their advice is worth hearing, partly because ignoring it may lead to facilities being cut off, but largely because they have seen many business failures and have learned a thing or two in the process. The bank manager knows that he will thrive if his customers do, but his first loyalty must necessarily lie with his employers. If he is placed in the position of having to choose between helping the customer and protecting the bank, his choice will be quite clear. The publicity put about in recent years about the banks' desire to help businesses is not untruthful. Many new services have been developed that are much more relevant to the needs of business than those offered a couple of decades ago. Many bank managers have been educated in the mysteries of management accounting, to give them a greater insight into the principles of how their customers operate their businesses. Despite all this valuable work, the eternal verities of banking have not changed, and probably never will.

At the most basic level, banking is done on the same principles as one would use when lending a virtual stranger £50. Assuming it was not meant as an act of charity, one would want to know what the money was to be used for, and would lend it only if one approved of the purpose. Furthermore, one would want to know what plans existed to repay it, but, above all, (this being only a stranger), one would want some security, his watch or some other possession. If he protested that his reputation and the practicality of his repayment plan were security enough, one might reply that they helped the loan to be made but were not themselves decisive. Similarly, the bank manager must protect the bank first, and his advice will be slanted accordingly. Mercifully, bank managers come in many shapes and sizes, and there may be a choice of advice on offer as well as the choice of promises of service.

Advice agencies

Some sixty years ago, Lloyd George set up the first British government organisation designed to advise and help small businesses. In recent years a host of organisations has appeared offering similar services, and the provision of advice to small firms has been one of Britain's few growth industries. It is worth seeking out exactly what the different organisations can do, for they all have their own particular strengths. First, the obvious distinction between them is that they employ different individuals. Some of these people are very competent and highly motivated, while others are less so. The smoothest-looking organisations do not necessarily employ the best people, and among the national agencies there can be noticeable local or regional variations. Another difference is in their constitution and objectives. Some may exist to promote employment with little knowledge of, or interest in, the wider needs of business. Others are there primarily to unload a local authority's unlet factories. Most exist to serve small firms by helping them to reach their objectives.

Business consultants

Finally, there is the world of business consultants. At one end of the spectrum are giant, international firms, at the other, individuals with some skill or knowledge that they seek to sell. The individual operators can be excellent, and they can be mere covers for insurance sales or finance house agencies, or worse. The larger firms are usually very good indeed and observe the highest professional standards. Unfortunately, they are expensive, and not in touch with the real world of the very small firm. There is no reason why they should be, for their living is earned elsewhere.

SECURITY OF INFORMATION

It is obvious that before any organisation or individual is invited to look at the firm's position their bona fides should be checked. A government or other public sector body's attitude to its clients' secrets can perhaps be taken for granted. The individual people who have responsibility within that organisation should be questioned, in order to determine whether they have any business interests that may be served by inside knowledge of the client's business, as well as to cover the obvious question of their suitability and qualifications to be dispensing advice. It may come as a surprise to learn that organisations in the public sector sometimes employ people who might be in a position to gain personally from information obtained in their professional capacity. It is no doubt unlikely that a businessman might unknowingly confide in a competitor, but accidents could happen and it would be wise to check. The same goes for accountants. Not everyone calling himself by that title is actually qualified and a member of a professional body which insists on high standards of conduct amongs its members. Again, a check is advised.

A private individual describing himself as a consultant obviously needs closer investigation still. Many of the better ones are senior managers who have taken early retirement, in which case they will have an employment history that they will be quite willing to reveal and have checked. These people have not only a considerable record of accomplishment which suggests that they know how to get things done, but often good business contacts in their former industry that can be useful to clients, and sometimes a small amount of capital that they might wish to invest in sound businesses with a good future. Someone of that type can be very helpful to many firms and sometimes eventually becomes a director or shareholder. It is obviously important that he should have some moral principles for, if they are lacking, he might be so plausible as to gain the owner's trust and have the technical understanding of how to relieve him of his business. Usually people of that type have a history that is known in the local professional and business community, so checks with the bank, accountant and solicitor are advisable. The firm may even take up credit agency checks and bank references, as well as having its solicitor approve the form of any agreement to involve the consultant more permanently. There may be no record to show he is only about to start his life of duplicity, so stringent checking of his whole story is important.

Consultants as decision-makers

The individual consultant may have one major attraction,

decisiveness. The professional adviser, however, will frequently seek to have the client decide, limiting himself to explaining the position and outlining the implications of the various courses of action that are possible. People often complain of this 'on the one hand ... on the other hand ...' approach. To do so is to misunderstand the professional's true role. His task is to bring his specialised technical knowledge of his field to bear on the situation in hand, and to outline options. He may extend that to offering an opinion of the probability of success or failure, and the costs attendant on each one. Only when very little is at stake or in really black-and-white situations will the issue be so straightforward as to make it possible for him to give single-option advice. In doing so, he is very probably recognising the right of the client to make the ultimate decision, because the client is the one who bears responsibility for the outcome.

The enormous load on owners of most small firms tempts some to use a consultant as a trusted colleague on whom responsibility for a whole department's activity can gradually be loaded. The dangers of this are obvious. When someone with no service agreement, or other formal commitment to the firm, personally controls one of its key areas there is fertile ground for mischief. If his responsibility is for manufacturing, the chance exists for a variety of corrupt or fraudulent methods to be used to transfer wealth from the firm to his own pocket. If he controls sales he could take away all the customers at a stroke, or at least enough of them to hurt. This is also an argument against relying on an outside sales organisation, incidentally. Needless to say, members of consultants' professional organisations would violate their professional codes if they behaved thus, but not all consultants are members, and to confuse matters further, membership does not guarantee excellence of performance.

Staff attitudes to consultants

Before deciding to take on an adviser, apart from the usual professional ones, the owner of the firm should give thought to his staff's attitudes. Consultants are often derided for charging one for repeating what one said to them. It may be worth thinking whether or not one of the existing staff could take on the assignment, possibly as the sole source of advice, possibly before the consultant is brought in. Whether or not his ideas agree with the consultant's, the owner will know more as a result. If the subordinate's ideas are altogether inferior he might perhaps learn from the exercise.

However it is done, the staff will suspect the consultant and look behind his appointment for sinister reasons. Their inclination to cooperate will vary. The professional consultant knows and expects all this and will raise these matters when discussing the assignment. He should have the ability quickly to gain the cooperation, if not the confidence, of the staff. Ideally, the boss will be able to tell his staff the true reasons for the consultant's involvement. In some circumstances he will wish to conceal part or all of the truth. He should do so only in the most dire circumstances, for it risks damaging irrevocably his staff's sense of commitment to him and to the firm. People can take bad news surprisingly well, and know instinctively that a particular department is in trouble. They can even be glad that at last something is being done to sort out the troublesome area, and welcome the consultant even though they think something personally unpleasant is almost certain to be the outcome.

Sources of advice

The main forms of advice available and advisers who specialise in helping small UK firms are described below.

THE SMALL FIRMS SERVICE (SFS)

This offshoot of the Department of Trade and Industry started life late in the 1960s as an information service on the end of a telephone. It now has regional offices (Small Firms Centres) which continue that work, as well as employing part time several hundred people with business experience to give general advice to small firms. It also publishes free booklets on various aspects of business. The advisers — Small Firms Counsellors — are drawn from the retired, and people operating their own businesses but with time on their hands. Some have highly distinguished careers behind them, and the continuing involvement in business of others must ensure that the advice given is up-to-date.

SFS can be contacted by dialling 100 and asking for freefone 2444. It does not advise the professions, nor agricultural and horticultural firms. All telephoned information is free of charge and the counsellors' services are free for the first few sessions, but are charged for thereafter at an hourly rate. SFS operates throughout Britain, and the Department of Commerce in

Northern Ireland operates a similar service.

SCOTTISH DEVELOPMENT AGENCY,
WELSH DEVELOPMENT AGENCY,
NORTHERN IRELAND DEVELOPMENT AGENCY

These quite separate organisations offer consulting and advisory services, and can lend money. They are also empowered to finance businesses by buying their shares. In addition, they advertise the countries they represent overseas to attract incoming industry and promote export sales. Their property connections add another dimension to their extensive service to the growing firm: they can help it to come into being, help finance its growth, house it, and help it to sell its wares. Furthermore, they will act as guides through the maze of grants and aid available in the differing parts of their areas.

To the growing firm already in an area covered by a Development Agency, their usefulness can readily be recognised. They are very professional at selling the idea of relocation, but the reality behind such airy attempts to minimise their physical distance from a firm's present location should be looked at hard. 'Only 140 minutes from London' really means one spends over four hours on the round trip that may take only one hour at present. It does not allow for factors like the firm's drivers running out of legally-permitted driving time on the motorway in winter. To say this is not to decry the Development Agencies' efforts or the quality of their proposition, but rather to say that relocation is a serious matter with implications favourable and unfavourable for every aspect of the firm's operations. Addresses appear in Appendix 4.

LOCAL AUTHORITIES, ENTERPRISE AGENCIES

Local authorities' attitudes to helping small firms vary widely. To find out if any help is available in a particular area, the quickest routes are probably to check with the public library and the national agencies, and to phone the economic development department of the authority concerned. If they seem to lack one, the planning department is probably the next best bet for information.

Some local authorities are setting up so-called Enterprise Agencies in partnership with industry. The idea seems to be to create institutions which will enable industry to help itself as well as allowing local government to contribute in a way that is less subject to the day-to-day vagaries of politics.

SUCCESSFUL EXPANSION

COUNCIL FOR SMALL INDUSTRIES IN RURAL AREAS (CoSIRA) Formerly the Rural Industries Bureau, CoSIRA has been operating in one form or another since the 1920s. It comes under the Development Commission, a government body which is part of the Department of the Environment.

The aims of CoSIRA are to revitalise the economic life of rural England by helping its small firms. Its local offices cover every English county (it does not operate outside England), staffed by people responsible for giving general business advice and knowing the local scene. They work to a policy jointly agreed between their independent county committee and CoSIRA's head office, and are able to call on about 100 full-time technical and management specialist staff to give help in depth. The specialists cover such areas as financial planning, marketing, production management, employment contracts, computerisation, building and planning permission, engineering, woodworking, plastics and much else besides. CoSIRA runs many short skills courses and one- and two-day management courses, as well as doing much work behind the scenes to further the cause of small firms in rural areas. In addition it can organise loan packages and also knows about grants and factory premises.

CoSIRA is available to firms employing fewer than 21 skilled employees (there is no limit to the number of unskilled) operating in communities of up to 10,000 population. It can help manufacturers, servicing firms, village stores, and some tourism-based businesses. No charge is made for work done by county officers, but specialists may be charged for at a few pounds per hour. They can be found in the phone book or, in case of difficulty, contacted through the head office, the address of which appears in Appendix 4.

AGRICULTURAL DEVELOPMENT AND ADVISORY SERVICE (ADAS) As the name suggests, these are the specialist advisers to the agricultural and horticultural industries. They are a branch of the Ministry of Agriculture, Fisheries and Food which appears in the phone book in most country areas.

Some people expect them to be exclusively involved with the problems of the big-acreage, intensive agri-businesses, but they are also very concerned to help the smaller establishment. Like the other government bodies, their services are either free or heavily subsidised.

ADVICE AND ADVISERS

CHAMBERS OF COMMERCE
Membership of its local chamber of commerce is very desirable for the growing firm. Their boards of directors can be dominated by representatives of large firms, but they are concerned to serve small firms as well, and offer some very useful services. Since they are all independent bodies, the exact menu offered by each varies, but in general the benefits will usually include advice on and certification of export documents, use of telex and a commercial reference library, newsletters giving details of business opportunities, and access to a large number of local business contacts. They are also very active in seeking to influence political leaders in favour of industry. Some of the larger chambers have very sophisticated services indeed.

HIGHER EDUCATIONAL INSTITUTIONS
Ranging from colleges of higher education to polytechnics and universities, these bodies can be very helpful in many ways. Those with technical departments may be able to help with perfecting machines or processes, those having business schools may help with the development of business plans and improving methods and systems within the firm. Many will be only too pleased to meet someone who can present students with real-life problems to work on. These students, who presumably go on to work in industry in many cases, will find it of great value to deal with questions that need solutions within a budget and to a timetable, rather than in an academic context where industrial disciplines rarely intrude. In turn, it may be very interesting to the firm to let a young tiger or two loose on its problems, especially if the cost is low because it is educational rather than consultancy work.

Many of the more enlightened institutions have formed small business units to make their strengths and abilities more available. Any small firm within the catchment area of one of them should lose no time in making contact to see what is offered. Usually it will be a combination of subsidised consultancy of high quality, introduction to other useful people and firms, and a programme of management courses. Some act as organisers of their local small business group, and few of their staff seem to take their full holiday entitlements. Their charges will vary according to the service given and the person giving it, averaging between £100 and £200 per day.

SUCCESSFUL EXPANSION

TOURIST BOARDS
The English, Welsh, Scottish and Northern Ireland Tourist Boards give advice to and run courses for tourism-based businesses. They also have a range of publications on various aspects of the management and promotion of tourism businesses, and a wealth of research information on tourism matters. Their publicity and marketing specialists will work mainly to promote tourism overall within their area, but are also available to advise individual firms.

SMALL FIRMS TECHNICAL ADVICE SERVICE
The Production Engineering Research Association (PERA) runs a government-aided programme called The Small Firms Technical Advice Service. It provides free consultancy for up to five days and subsidised help thereafter. Its main strengths are, as would be expected, in engineering. The contact point is given in Appendix 4.

GOVERNMENT RESEARCH AND DEVELOPMENT (R&D) HELP
Some of the help given by government to industry's R&D has threshold expenditures that put it out of the reach of small firms. However, several schemes are particularly designed to help the smaller business, the main ones of which are listed in Appendix 4. As the list is constantly changing, it is worth checking with the departments concerned, and also to ask the Small Firms Centre if there have been any recent additions.

One of the best ways of crippling a company is to fund R&D out of cash flow. What looks initially like a modest expenditure over a short period of time all too often develops into a long-term nightmare. It goes like this: the new product has absorbed so much time and effort that it must be finished to get back the investment; but the existing business has suffered through the diversion of effort, so time must be spent reviving it. Therefore, there will either be no new product and loss of the investment so far, or there will be no company at all.

Therefore a proper R&D programme should be drawn up at the outset and realistically costed, probably with advice from an accountant. The proposal can then be evaluated financially to see if the likely return is justified, and funded properly by a bank loan, possibly with help from a government grant.

Chapter 6
More of the Same, or Exciting New Products?

Expansion of a business usually means selling more, although there are rare examples of firms that steadily go further and further up-market, raising prices and profits without greatly increasing the amount of goods sold. The main point of an expansion, expressed in the firm's overall objective, will more often mean selling greater volumes of goods, while keeping prices as high as possible in the circumstances. This may be achieved by adding new products, or by selling greater volumes of the existing range, or, most likely, a combination of both. To speak of keeping prices as high as possible does not preclude a cut-price assault as a tactic, merely to recognise that in such a situation prices would not be cut beyond the point where sufficient return was earned. Sales volume alone does not equal cash flow and profit, yet cash flow and profit keep firms alive.

Existing products, present markets

In choosing how to add volume, the most profitable method for most firms is the most humdrum: selling more of the existing products to the existing markets. It may not have the glamour and excitement attached to launching new products or attacking new markets, but it has greater profit potential. It is probably true to say that most firms are operating at less than saturation of their current markets. 'Saturation' here does not mean a 100 per cent market share, but the level beyond which it costs more to get the extra sale than the profit it brings in. It is often difficult for the people directly involved with the situation to see how they could do better, and in fairness it should be said that perhaps their ideas have been pursued vigorously and to the maximum effect. There may be opportunities which will be unearthed only by the involvement of an outsider bringing his different perspectives and experience to bear. Equally, new ideas can be generated by the simple process of looking at the company's present methods and questioning them. If it distributes only within a 30-mile radius, need this be so, or can it expand to 50 miles? Doing that, incidentally, would more than double the geographical area served, though not necessarily the number of potential customers. Self-criticism may or may not prove to be the company's most effective generator of new ideas, but it will almost certainly be the cheapest.

The manner in which self-criticism is conducted is important. If it is used merely as an excuse for the boss or other employees to complain about the current low level of ideas in the firm, the people who feel criticised will take up defensive positions and little will be gained. If, on the other hand, a number of people are invited to address the problem of how the firm as a whole can achieve its aim, a more positive response can be expected. The question of creative thinking is explored further in Chapter 8.

New products, new markets

Many firms on the expansion trail go straight into developing a new product. It is highly seductive, this idea of starting with a blank piece of paper and designing the one perfect product which will sweep the market and make the firm's fortune. In the more technically advanced industries it is almost a matter of pride to push back the frontiers of knowledge, and the boss who tries to get his staff to work on existing technology risks their scorn. All this is a problem for the owner because most of the firms which survive and make money tend to be the exploiters of technology rather than its inventors. Thus, the least profitable projects upon which companies embark can be those in which they sell new products to new markets.

These are guidelines rather than immutable rules, but they carry enough weight to justify the businessman thinking carefully about whether or not the principles involved apply to his pet project. The main reasons for the high risks seem to be:

– Insufficient appreciation of the time needed to develop new products
– Unforeseen snags in development leading to delay and extra expense
– Temptation to over-engineer leading to excessive cost
– Insufficient improvement over products currently available
– Delayed launch loses the hoped-for lead over competitors
  Over-optimistic initial appreciation of the market

MORE OF THE SAME, OR EXCITING NEW PRODUCTS?

- Inexperience of the market leading to false assumptions over key questions
- Inability to devote enough time to selling the new product
- Hazarding the existing business by diverting more and more productive time to research and development.

At the start of a project to develop a new product it can appear easy to foresee its timetable and the amount of involvement likely to be called for. In practice, the old rule of the pessimistic accountant often applies: think of a number, then double it. It is therefore advisable to prepare a budget for the project before starting on it. The results could be surprising, and sobering. This question is covered in detail in Chapter 8. It is critically important, for so many firms have driven themselves out of business by unplanned new product development. They seem to get carried along by the challenge of problem-solving, which is so much more fun than running the ordinary business. A blind spot develops about the need to do less exciting work in order to pay the bills.

If developing a new product is absolutely unavoidable, it is often better to create it for a known market than for one in which the firm has no experience. The dire warning about the pitfalls still applies, but one major area will be more predictable. The real needs of customers will be better known, the firm will know where they are and how to sell to them, and will probably have useful sales contacts. Best of all, if the new product sells to the same customers as the existing range, it should not only carve out its own niche in the market but also help to increase sales of the more established products. It has the effect of helping the firm to present a more comprehensive range, making it more credible as a supplier.

New product, present markets

In some cases it is better for the firm to develop a new product for its existing markets, and in others to sell its existing range to new markets. It depends on many factors, chief among them being how the firm is able to respond to the requirements of the different markets available to it. It would be difficult for a tanker haulage specialist to break into the express parcels market. Although he knows everything about running and maintaining a transport fleet, the critical factor in express parcels is speedy, flexible and efficient handling and communications systems, capable of working reliably under high pressure. The technology and management skills of running a vehicle fleet are not unimportant, but are secondary.

The maker of small power tools for specialised applications in industry might develop a wonderful new product for the home handyman, but he will find it difficult to sell because reaching that kind of customer is beyond his ability. If he is to take on Black & Decker, Bosch, and others, he will need to offer the same universal availability of spares and service, to say nothing of advertising, point-of-sale displays, and a professional consumer-goods sales force. It might be better for him to offer further new products to his existing market or, if he must venture into new fields, to extend his approach to small tradesmen — plumbers, electricians, builders, and the like — rather than the general public. They are relatively cheap and easy to reach by direct mail, telephone sales or personal contact, using Yellow Pages to provide lists. They might want an up-rated and toughened version, but at least the task of selling to them is not wholly out of tune with the firm's skills, nor out of scale with its resources.

Another mismatch of scale occurs if the small firm does pull off the legendary order from Woolworths, and finds that it will take three months to make the quantity required for delivery in three weeks' time. One might think that nobody would ever make a mistake as obvious as that, nor commit the other fundamental errors described above, but it happens every day in large firms and small ones alike. It must therefore be the result of some basic human failing. In the large firm it may be due to middle management people desperately seizing on some way of keeping their jobs, and in the small firm the hurly-burly of events stopping the owner from concentrating on the full implications of the issues. Whatever the cause, the result is usually very similar. Much effort, time and tangible resources are wasted, and after the inevitable failure, bad feeling is caused by the recriminatory hunt for scapegoats.

Therefore, by far the least risky course in the short term, if it can be achieved, is to sell more of the present range to the present market. In the longer term it may be necessary to update products and develop new ones, but most firms could get much more out of their present product range if they tried.

Ways and Means

If that statement is made to hard-working salesmen they are inclined to knot their brows and belligerently ask just how the speaker thinks it can be done. It all depends, of course, on where the opportunity lies. The main areas for consideration are:

- ☐ Sales force effectiveness: training, organisation, management
- ☐ New customer identification: analysis of opportunities, setting objectives
- ☐ Sales promotion: inducements to customers and users
- ☐ After-sales service: guarantees, service agreements, trade-ins
- ☐ Other non-product factors: finance, credit, delivery.

Only after the owner is satisfied that these matters have been explored as deeply as possible should he feel that he needs to tinker with the product itself.

SALES FORCE CONTROL

Few salesmen can honestly say that they have a planned programme for picking off the primary sales prospects in their territories; most meander on from visit to visit, spending an undue amount of time on the calls where they get a sympathetic hearing or a cup of tea. And who can blame them? Selling is a lonely life, cut off from the normal working relationships that most people enjoy, exposed to rebuff after rebuff, and full of the worry that three weeks' missed targets will lead to the sack. Small wonder that, if their firm lets them get away with it, some salesmen carry additional, commission-only lines to sell in their employer's time.

Tight control of what salesmen do is even more essential than with other staff. Lorry drivers know that the tell-tale tachograph will give clues to any misbehaviour, factory staff risk being seen if they skulk in corners, but salesmen are often quick-witted and articulate enough to cover their tracks, and they are away on their own nearly all of the time. To ensure that they do what they are paid for, it is good practice to have them submit a weekly plan showing their future activity.

This will cause the salesman to think ahead, with the benefits that he will plan his days to spend as little time as possible driving, follow a logical sequence of calls, and commit himself to at least a minimum amount of calling on new prospects.

SUCCESSFUL EXPANSION

Salesman's Call Plan
Week Commencing: .... Name: .... Week No: .....
Sun
Mon
Tue
Wed
Thur
Fri
Sat
NB. Bracket prospective customers' names

Without this sort of pre-planning it is too tempting for him to get in the car on a cold Monday morning and automatically drive where he will get a pleasant reception. Once that pattern is established, it is difficult to break.

The call plan can be returned for revision if it is inadequate in any way, but it also serves to compare with the weekly report of what was actually achieved. Knowledge of that fact keeps the salesman's concentration on the job in hand, including the need to call on awkward as well as pleasant people. That weekly report will include the following information:

- ☐ Which customers the salesman has visited
- ☐ The category of each customer or prospect
- ☐ The outcome of the call
- ☐ Further action required.

Some call reports also require analysis of results and comparison with target, times and durations of visits, and daily mileages. Having the salesman analyse his own performance and compare it with target is a good way of jolting him into taking the necessary corrective action.

Important though it is to ensure that salesmen are organising their work well and calling according to plan, the quality of what goes on during each visit also matters. Many training organisations offer short courses for salesmen to improve their skills, and it may be worth using one to complement and amplify the in-company training. They will also audit the current performance before recommending training, if requested, but this will cost money. Some of the public-sector organisations mentioned in Appendix 4 may be able to offer the auditing service at much lower cost.

FINDING POTENTIAL CUSTOMERS
Sometimes the buyer makes it really simple, by advertising in newspapers and trade journals an invitation to tender. Public bodies are the most frequent users of this method.

In more conventional markets it is easy to identify potential customers, and in others very difficult indeed. The firm selling small electric motors knows which manufacturers incorporate its products in their output and can approach them accordingly; stockists and repairers of electric motors are another obvious target. All are fairly easy to find and to approach: ten minutes with trade directories and Yellow Pages will yield many prospective customers. On the other hand, a supplier to a more diffuse market has a more difficult job, made worse if his product is bought only occasionally. An example might be a carpet supplier.

He knows that at any one time there is a certain demand for his service, but his first task is to make sure that his salesmen are invited to quote. He does not know who is likely to be considering the replacement carpets, so how does he tackle the problem? His salesmen will probably be required to comb the newspapers and listen to local radio and TV news for information on fires, floods, and other calamities that befall shops, offices and other establishments that cannot afford to close down for lengthy refits. They may cultivate contacts among the police and fire service, so as to be the first on the scene for renovation work (in the USA this is picturesquely known as 'ambulance chasing'). Less gruesomely, they will cultivate contacts with those responsible for accommodation at large firms and public-sector institutions, so that they might be included on tendering lists, or invited to quote when replacement work is due. To stimulate this type of work they might offer free surveys to check on the state of flooring from the point of view of safety regulations. They will also cultivate the industrial and commercial property sector, builders and property agents, to be sure of quoting for firms that are expanding or new to the area. All of that can be done by salesmen without a penny of expense on advertising. The market for domestic carpets is quite different, and is normally

SUCCESSFUL EXPANSION

approached by means of showrooms and advertising.

ADVERTISING, SALES PROMOTION AND PUBLICITY
Although some of the work can be done virtually unaided by salesmen, some needs head office support. It will do no harm if the electric motor users, the builders, the property managers, and so on, receive communications from HQ from time to time, and it might even help the salesmen to be more effective. Such communications can be in the form of advertisements in the trade and local press, direct mail (sales letters and brochures sent by post), invitations to exhibitions, press articles, and many more. It is easy to spend large amounts of money on advertising, much of which can be wasted.

Advertising, direct mail and exhibitions are all facets of the wider field of promoting sales. Advertising is traditionally thought of as being directed to long-term ends, and the other activities, lumped together as 'sales promotion', towards short-term goals. The important thing is that they should all be:

- ☐ Clear to the audience they address
- ☐ Consistent in tone, content and appearance
- ☐ Aimed at achieving defined objectives
- ☐ Capable of having their effects measured.

In some industries the major part of the advertising budget is spent on advertisements, in some on exhibitions, and in others on promotional offers, and so on. Sometimes it pays to join the crowd, sometimes the winner is the one who breaks the supposed rules. There can be no hard-and-fast general rule for success, except perhaps that advertising and promotion are tools for doing a particular job, and their effectiveness in doing it should, as far as possible, be measured. To carry that to an extreme would be wrong, for some valuable aspects of advertising are virtually impossible to measure, but it would also be wrong to make no attempt at all to determine effectiveness. A further aspect of advertising that is often overlooked is that it must usually be repetitive to be really effective. There are exceptions, of course, where the one-off ad does work, but most of the time at least five or six repetitions are necessary before an ad has been given a fair chance.

While advertising is the mass-communication medium that naturally springs first to mind, there are others. The one most neglected by small firms is editorial publicity. Few people realise that much of what is written in trade magazines and local papers was not the product of a zealous journalist's investigation, but was written by the organisation itself and sent out as a press release. Anyone unfamiliar with the rules for writing and presenting them should consult their marketing and publicity adviser.

The more advertising is specifically addressed to the buyer, the more effective it is. In those markets where buyers are known by name, the telephone and direct mail can be used to supplement the salesman's efforts, or even replace him altogether. Elsewhere a hybrid arrangement can be tried, using the telephone and the sales letter to contact all potential customers and select for personal visits only those who show some interest in buying. These ways of weeding out uninterested customers can make the expensive salesman far more productive.

A great many markets are governed by specifications over which manufacturers have no control. An example might be items provided by the National Health Service on a doctor's prescription, rigidly specified by the government department concerned. It is not impossible to imagine a situation where manufacturers could see that the Civil Service specification might be designed to protect the government from criticism, rather than to provide the user with the most comfortable product. The result might be a product that lasts forever, but is hopelessly over-engineered, heavy and ungainly, costing far more than the more comfortable non-prescription item. Restrictions on government spending mean that it is worth the manufacturer's while to offer the department an alternative design which will be more friendly to the user, whilst enabling the shrinking budgets to go further. Civil servants can be influenced although the process is often a long one, and even if they show little interest in value for money, their political masters are usually more receptive.

New products for old

So far, discussion of new products has centred around the creation of something involving true innovation in the manufactured item itself. But there are other, less costly, ways of attracting attention which do not involve tinkering with the manufacturing technology of the existing product. Look at the product from the point of view of the customer and consider all its characteristics, except the technical ones, with a view to making them more attractive.

SUCCESSFUL EXPANSION

The variables include:

Pack. Size, material, reusable, disposable, shape, multi-pack, gift-pack

Appearance. Styling, finish, economy, luxury, practical, decorative

After sales. Speed of delivery, service, guarantee, trade-in, spares, second-hand value

Uses. New uses, alternative uses, customised specification

Finance. Instalment purchase, credit, leasing

Channels of distribution. Direct sales, party plan, shows, wholesalers, retailers, mail order

Price. High, low, points between.

This list is far from comprehensive, but taken together with all the methods of promoting sales, it constitutes what is called the 'marketing mix'. The ideal to which the businessman aims is to have the most efficient marketing mix possible — the one which achieves most output for least input. It is a useful notion as it prompts one to see that the elements that go to make it up are interdependent. High-priced products will tend to make high margins, but they must not be excessively eroded by the costs of promotion and dealer training support which may be necessary to sell their benefits and justify their price. Low-priced products on tight margins will have to be sold by big customers in large volumes if they are to pay for the advertising support that those customers may demand, and still leave some profit over; or a lot of money may be spent on very special packaging and point-of-sale material and little on advertising. Whatever the marketing mix, the test of the businessman is the figure on the bottom line, the profit or — perish the thought — loss.

PRICING

Pricing is a topic which many small business people find it difficult to come to terms with. They recognise that all their overheads and other costs must be met, but do not dare to charge the price that logic dictates. 'Our customers won't put up with that', is their cry. So be it, if they are prepared to accept a life of penury and possible business failure. The ambitious owner cannot adopt this stance. He accepts the logic of his costs and the need for healthy profits, and does one of two things: either he puts up prices and stresses the product's benefits in order to keep existing customers or find new ones, or he cuts his costs in order to improve margins. There is no other way for him to achieve his desires.

THE CUSTOMER'S FINANCIAL PACKAGE
Where items with a large unit cost are concerned, the benefits of the product itself may be no more important — or even less — than the financial package that enables them to be bought. At one end of the spectrum this may mean that the small manufacturer who sells items for £20 at agricultural and other shows gets business if he takes credit cards, but not if he accepts only cash. However desirable and affordable the product may be, if customers do not carry a spare £20 they cannot buy it for cash.

On a grander scale there is the agricultural machinery supplier who gives his farmer customers a choice. They can have discounts for cash immediately, or they can pay full price when they have been paid for their harvest. The danger is that the latter may often attract the worst credit-risks, but there can be checks on customers' creditworthiness before acceptance of orders.

NEW CHANNELS OF DISTRIBUTION
A change of distribution channels can greatly affect the fortunes of a company, or indeed an entire industry. Some prime examples are Tupperware, Avon Cosmetics and Snap-On Tools. The 'rules' that they broke were that polythene household goods were sold by hardware shops, cosmetics were sold only by chemists and department stores, and professional mechanics' tools by motor and general engineering stockholders. They had the vision to see how the ultimate consumer could be better served if they dealt direct with him or her, and the rest is dazzlingly successful history. Tupperware virtually founded the party-plan style of selling, since taken up by so many other businesses; Avon have taken a huge share of the cosmetics market; and Snap-On's mobile stockrooms mean that mechanics and engineers can see the full range available and try them before they buy. All three firms also have a reputation for scrupulous attention to quality, which enables them to justify their high prices, presumably also providing healthy margins.

EXPORTING
In the race to expand, exporting can look very tempting. It can be an excellent move for some firms, but those who succeed at it have to work even harder at developing overseas markets than they do at home. Not all of those who work hard succeed, so

the risks are high. To cap it, the fluctuations in exchange rates between foreign currencies and sterling can wipe out what looked like a healthy profit at the time of taking the order.

The marketing difficulties can be more easily imagined if a reverse example is cited. How credible would an Italian (say) seem if he tried to sell something to an English firm? The language barrier, difficulties over understanding each other's normal commercial practice and the fear that, if something went wrong with the deal, getting satisfaction from a foreign firm nearly 1000 miles away might be difficult. If, on top of that, he insisted on quoting in lira he would make a hard task nearly impossible. That is not to say that exporting is impossible, but that to succeed it is necessary, not just to be as good as the foreign-based competitor, but to be better. If the days ever existed when the British were forgiven for amateurishness in export markets, they are certainly gone now. Some British products — Scotch whisky and Burberry coats, for instance — have an undeniable cachet for being British, but the exporters know that they cannot afford to assume that it licenses them to behave as less than full professionals. The company that is best placed to export is the one with strong home sales. In no way can exporting be looked on as a way of unloading products that the British will not buy.

A useful way of testing a product's acceptability in export markets is to offer it to the UK-based buyers for overseas department stores, and to the confirming houses. This route also avoids personal involvement with foreign markets, and therefore cuts out a lot of the inconvenience and risk of selling abroad. Not every product is suitable to be sold in this way, but the government and private sector export advisers will give guidance and make introductions.

If the firm does go ahead with exporting it will do well to consult its chamber of commerce and the British Overseas Trade Board (BOTB), both of whom can give practical help and advice. The bank will help to explain the different payment conventions and procedures, and cover for risks. As much information as possible on the prospective market should be assembled, especially in the fields of local banking, and any exchange and import controls and, of course, local law. Not only will BOTB help with local knowledge, but will make introductions to the British Embassy (which has a trade attaché responsible for promoting our exports). At the home end of the chain, it is worth checking all proposals with the importing country's embassy or high commission for advice on one's resulting liabilities or responsibilities.

As with the home market, export salesmen or overseas-based agents need to be properly briefed, trained and controlled. They must be very clear about what the firm will accept in dealing with customers and what it will not. Exporting complicates the picture, particularly where there are language differences, because of the peculiar insurance, credit, exchange, transport and contract arrangements, so there are policies to construct. It would be foolish to leave decisions on such vital matters to the agent. He may be involved in assessing credit risks and collecting payments, and once again needs unequivocal statements of policy to follow. It must be quite clear to all parties, exporter, agent, and customer, exactly who is responsible for what at every stage of the sale and afterwards.

Chapter 7
Expanding by Takeover

A takeover looks like a quick way to instant growth. All that needs to be done is to find a firm that is compatible with the present set-up, buy it up, and bolt them together. It can work, but like so many other obvious ideas it has its pitfalls. Because the stakes are usually higher, the penalties for the wrong move are that much heavier.

What is on offer?

As in every other business decision it is important for the acquisition to be part of the overall business plan. Unrepeatable opportunities are always worth a look, but should be proceeded with only if they match the business's overall needs and only if they pass the most stringent and searching investigation. If there is no time for the investigation, or not enough time for it to be thorough, the chance should perhaps pass to a more reckless buyer, or one who is better prepared. It might prove to be a good chance lost but, more often than not, the more eager buyer is the sort of optimist who buys a used car from a dealer with a string of convictions for fraud.

There is obviously no point in buying a business far removed from the existing one. It must match it, and should complement it. The very large firm may be able to justify different sorts of businesses under one top management, but the small firm rarely can. A close look at the big multi-division business often shows its holding company at arm's length from the operating firm, each of which is run almost independently. The holding company does little more than act as banker and motivator. Its takeover decisions can be based on purely financial calculations, though a match with the group's existing businesses can be a bonus. Or it might not, if the idea is to diversify away from over-dependence on one sector. In the small firm such dilemmas are rare. For an acquisition even to be considered as an option it must offer the chance speedily to overcome the barriers to growth. If they can be better overcome by some other method, acquisition should be discarded as a possibility.

Having identified what the business needs in order to expand, a profile of the ideal acquisition almost defines itself. If the business needs better access to markets, the takeover target which is strong only in manufacturing becomes unattractive, and the more market-effective subject only is considered. It is usually not the function of the acquisition to buttress existing strengths, but to strengthen areas of weakness.

Identifying possible acquisitions

Preparing the profile of the ideal company to be taken over is the first step. Next, the owner's knowledge of his market and competitors comes into play to tell him which firms are likely to fit the profile. If they are approached in the right way, suppliers and customers can offer a great deal of information, supplementing other sources. These can include inspecting local trade directories, making enquiries of local trade associations and chambers of commerce, being inquisitive at exhibitions, keeping an eye on trade press reports and advertising, and noting personnel changes and their implications. Thus a dossier can be compiled on each possible victim.

Sometimes firms come on to the market in an orderly way, particularly when an owner in good health decides to retire. More often, they are offered unexpectedly, perhaps due to some personal tragedy, or to a cash crisis. It is then that the studious research done previously comes into its own. The acquiring company that has done its homework can make a considered offer before others have even absorbed the news. Disclosure of the long-term gathering of facts can secure the bank's help by showing that it is not an opportunist purchase, but one that has been planned. It is more likely to win than another firm that can show the bank only a sale agent's or receiver's brochure, facts unchecked, and demand an immediate decision.

Part of the process of identification is an assessment of the people needed to run the victim firm. The plan may depend on keeping their existing people on — how is this to be achieved, and how are they to be controlled? Or it might assume that they will not be needed, in which case redundancy and retirement costs may be incurred. These can be particularly burdensome if directors and senior staff have fixed-term

SUCCESSFUL EXPANSION

contracts. A misleading piece of quasi-economic theory is that 'more means cheaper': that putting two firms together must automatically lead to savings. Unfortunately, it does not follow. As many sadder, poorer, and wiser businessmen will attest, where sales are concerned two plus two often equals three; as for costs, two plus two can equal five or more. The assumption may be made that only one accounts department is needed, yet it might be impossible to implement because conventions and methods differ greatly; or it may be thought that the production of both firms can be fitted into the factory of one — that may be true, but perhaps the other factory is unsaleable, so that the expected cash return cannot be obtained. These are only two of the many assumptions made in haste and repented for so long afterwards by many firms. Yet again, the only way to avoid the pitfalls is to think through its full implications really thoroughly before the decision is taken.

Putting competitors into business

It is not unknown for the businessman who has never before effected a takeover to be so excited by a successful outcome that he displays a good deal of arrogance to the staff of the company he has acquired. His excitement is entirely understandable, but insensitivity towards his new employees may well rebound on him very hard indeed.

The staff will, naturally, be anxious about their positions. They know that takeovers are often the preliminary to wholesale sackings. If those fears are unjustified they should be told within hours of the announcement being made public, otherwise the key employees may be rapidly lost. Assuming the worst, they will not wait for the official word, but will immediately begin to apply for jobs. Some may even need only to phone back the firm that has been trying to head-hunt them for months; others may know of other, local, jobs for which they need only apply to be accepted. To maximise the inconvenience, it will be the key staff, the best and indispensable people, who go most quickly, because they are the ones most in demand elsewhere.

This series of events deals the new owner a double blow. Not only can he not run his new acquisition as he would wish, except by diverting scarce management time, but his competitors have recruited people who know more about his new business than he does. Or, most formidable of all, his key managers break away to set up their own firm using the know-how he has paid dearly for.

Thus, a little charm and, if possible, a clear announcement of intentions, will go a long way in the early hours of the takeover. If there are to be mass sackings, no false promises should be made, but it would be wise to speak privately with the key people to assure them that they have a future with the firm whatever the position of colleagues. Even that has its dangers, for people will be on the look-out for unusual activity involving the new owners and will form fairly accurate conclusions, which ignorance will embroider into something quite unlike their true intentions.

It is important to remember that for the first six months at least of the new regime, key people will regard their new masters as being on trial. Their commitment may appear to be high, for they naturally realise that they, too, must perform, but their emotional commitment, the sense that they belong here for the foreseeable future, may be missing. As a precaution they may make job applications that they do not really mean, except as an insurance against any unpleasantness. Thus the owner is faced by two distinct tasks: to get to know or have one of his staff get to know, quickly, as much of the jobs of key people as possible, while treating the new employees as full members of the team. Because the owner has read and followed the precepts outlined in Chapter 2, this means that the new staff will probably want to stay.

Another important aspect of potential competition is the possibility that the former owner might be tempted to set up a new firm with an almost identical name in the same line of business as the one he has just sold. The fact that this is plainly unfair would not deter some people, so the contract of sale needs to take this into account. It might not be realistic to ban the chap forever from operating in the only field he knows, and it might not be enforceable; but some sort of control, albeit limited, may be appropriate. A restaurateur may be barred from operating within a 20-mile radius for three years, say, or a manufacturer from operating at all for two years — a suitable formula is usually available that gives adequate protection to the new owners in the delicate early stages of the operation, while answering the seller's reasonable demand that he be allowed to earn his living.

If the seller is in good health and not committed elsewhere, he may consider an invitation to serve as a consultant for a defined period of time. This may be of any duration from one week to two years, the important thing being to keep him from possible mischief for a suitable length of time as well as ensuring a smooth hand-over. The period of consultancy will therefore be related to the new owner's assessment of the situation, not to mention the former owner's willingness to cooperate. If such an arrangement is contemplated it is important that two things are done: it should be mentioned in the contract of sale, and a consultancy agreement should be drawn up. These actions ensure that an element in the sale agreement is that the former owner will use his best endeavours to help the new management. If his help is half-hearted, or quite absent, retention of all or part of the agreed sale price may be justified. Knowing this, the seller will be keen to be useful. The function of the consultancy agreement is to define just what he is being employed for, for what hours, at what price, and so forth. By agreeing all this in advance, the risk of later misunderstandings and conflict is minimised.

Financial aspects

What is an acquisition worth? Most buyers will seek to pay as little as possible, sellers to extract as much as they can. Somehow, the laws of economics tell us, an equilibrium is arrived at which determines the one, true market price. Not for the first time, the laws of economics neatly summarise the final destination without actually telling anyone how to get there.

The answer differs for every enquirer, because the usefulness of the business will vary from buyer to buyer. Some might want only the premises and regard the fittings as things that they will have to pay someone to take away. Others will want only the sales outlets or the products, and expect to reduce the cost of their purchase by selling off surplus fixed assets. Not surprisingly, their calculations of value will differ.

Even so, the vendor may have an inflated view of the price he can get. There is often little that can be done in such a case, except to pay his price or wait for realism to dawn. Even the most professionally prepared valuation, embodying all sorts of clever investment appraisal techniques, can fall at this fence. The problem is usually in one of two categories. Either the seller needs a certain sum of money to finance his retirement or his next project, in which case he cannot accept less than his asking price or he will be left with insufficient funds. Or his

EXPANDING BY TAKEOVER

proper pride in his business has got out of proportion to the point where an offer lower than his figure is seen as a stinging insult. In neither case will rational argument prevail, and time and effort spent on it will be wasted.

Calculating the value of the investment, using standard accounting techniques, is more or less child's play. Whether or not it is worth the potential investor paying that figure, or more, or less, is a matter for the businessman's judgement in relation to the other options open to him. As for the standard techniques themselves, the most commonly used are:

PAYBACK

A cash flow forecast is constructed, incorporating assumptions about inflation. This method then looks at how long the project's net cash flow takes to recoup its original cost. If two or more options are being considered, this method will show, in the most favourable light, those likely to have the quickest payback. For the cash-hungry small firm operating in an uncertain environment it may be an appropriate method. It will not reflect accurately the effect of timing, nor the longer-term effects.

PRESENT VALUE

This method takes a different approach from the payback principle and overcomes its disadvantages. It recognises that £1 today is worth more than £1 in a year's time, because of interest, which the other methods mentioned here do not. In essence, it involves forecasting the project's cash flows and applying to them the effects of interest. It is worth taking two or three forecasts of interest rates and working out the arithmetic to see whether, and how, each would affect the proposal. Anyone who has access to a home computer could write a simple program for this, and might even make it more sophisticated by, for example, seeing what happens if interest rates rise or fall in the future rather than assuming the same rate throughout.

For simpler souls there exist discount tables which, ready-reckoner style, show that if interest is at 10 per cent, £1 today is worth 91p in a year's time, or 82p after two years, and so on; or the humble pocket calculator's 'constant' function can be set to the appropriate discount rate. To work out the discount rate for a given rate of interest, follow the formula overleaf.

SUCCESSFUL EXPANSION

$$\text{Discount rate} = \frac{100}{(100 + \text{interest rate})}$$

eg, if interest rate selected is 12½ per cent:

$$\text{Discount rate} = \frac{100}{(100 + 12\tfrac{1}{2})}$$

$$= \frac{100}{112\tfrac{1}{2}}$$

$$= 0.89$$

This shows that £1 today is worth 89p in a year's time. To calculate its worth in two year's time, multiply again by the discount rate, ie, 0.89 x 0.89 = 0.79; thus £1 two years hence is worth 79p in today's money, assuming 12½ per cent interest.

RETURN ON INVESTMENT
This involves calculating the average balance sheet value of the purchase over its expected life, and relating to it the average annual profit over the same period. Thus, if the assets to be acquired are valued at £20,000 and should last for five years, their average value is £20,000 divided by 5 = £4,000. If they earn £2,000 per year on average, the return on the investment is £2,000 divided by £4,000 = 50 per cent per year, which sounds marvellous. The alert reader will have spotted the trap, however: the time-value of money has been completely ignored. The averages disguise the differing present values of early or late returns from the project.

It may well be worth carrying out all these different calculations, not relying on one of them to be conclusive, but using each of them to illuminate the decision in its own special way. As was said earlier, investment decisions in large or small firms are rarely taken on accounting criteria alone, but this does not mean that they should be ignored. They can be particularly useful as aids to a sound decision when two options are being considered, for instance the possible takeover of one of two companies, or the question of buying a firm to eliminate an area of weakness as opposed to internally developing that missing strength over a period of time. Even when only one course of action is being considered it can be salutary to find that the financial effect is likely to be worse than putting the money in a bank deposit or somewhere equally safe. In such circumstances, the question will automatically, and rightly, arise about the true value of the intangible benefits that the takeover is expected to yield. Sometimes people feel that merely asking such questions is an attack on the idea itself. It is not. It is extending the range of consideration given to the decision, so that the scope for foolishness is reduced.

How to pay

Ways of raising finance for this, or any other, type of investment, are discussed in detail in Chapter 9, so here we shall go into only those areas that might form part of the sale agreement.

If there is any chance of doing so, it would obviously be best to spread payments over a period of time. This clearly reduces the amount of cash that needs to be raised, and enables the purchase to be funded out of the earnings that it contributes. If that is offered by the seller, or requested by the buyer, it would be reasonable for a higher price overall to be paid. To the buyer it might be a more helpful method, despite a higher price, as it will not affect his bank borrowing. He might also feel reassured over the information given by the seller about the performance of the business if he is in a position to withhold a large part of the sale price should it prove to be false or exaggerated. The buyer, on the other hand, would presumably prefer a cash deal, although he will be influenced by his tax position and the sheer availability, or otherwise, of an alternative offer. Not every business that comes on the market is immediately pursued by generous and wealthy suitors. Equally, not every business that comes on the market is seriously for sale at anything less than an unrealistically high price: the offer may only be meant to test the water to see if there is a rich fool around.

Caution, and hence deferred payments, are highly desirable. Very few well-managed firms with a good history and an apparently sound future ever come on to the open market. It may look like a good offer, but so did every single disastrous purchase ever made.

Some of the traps

A list of the unpleasant situations that people have uncovered after taking over a firm would be about as long as one of all the possible moves in chess. It will therefore not be attempted. A few of the more obvious ones, which even people intelligent enough to know better sometimes try on, are shown overleaf.

SUCCESSFUL EXPANSION

- Equipment is over-valued, possibly not maintained properly
- Seller plans to start up in competition, taking customers with him
- Market is on a down-trend
- Long-running contracts are about to expire and will not be renewed
- Redevelopment, local authority planning or rent reviews will affect the business
- New competitor is taking all the custom
- Stock is obsolete, non-existent, unsaleable, or otherwise over-valued
- Historically, sales were bolstered by undisclosed means: eg, a shop plus three market stalls — the shop is for sale and the records show all turnover going through it, which is strictly true, but the seller does not mention the market stalls which he will keep for himself.

This list is far from complete, but it does serve to stress the need for independent valuation, backed up by detailed prying into every aspect of the valuer's findings, as well as of the firm's environment and its alleged operations. Historical accounts will give clues to some factors, but those which have become significant only recently, or are expected to have an effect in the future, cannot be discovered either from old accounts or even the best valuation. Let the buyer beware!

Blending old and new

In theory, if the advice given so far has been followed, there will be little difficulty in putting the new acquisition together with the existing firm. It will all have been thought out so thoroughly in advance that no problem will arise that has not been foreseen and taken into account. As the reader, and even more so the writer, are but fallible humans, this is very unlikely indeed.

It would be unforgivable if an error had been made on the loftiest strategic plane. It is improbable that, say, a hotel has been bought instead of the engineering works that the firm really needed, and so the possibility will be ignored (although funnies of that type are sometimes perpetrated).

On a realistic level, the main problems are likely to be those concerning people and the conditions under which they work. They include:

- Harmonising compensation systems

- Unifying administration
- Mutual understanding of technology, systems, constraints and opportunities between what were formerly two distinct operating managements.

The first one is likely to be solved by a dictator-like decision. The new company's people are to be compensated on exactly the same basis as those in the original firm. This means not that they must be paid the same or be paid differently, but that the basis for calculation is the same for all, and seen to be so.

The second question deserves careful thought. On the one hand the newly acquired firm has developed systems related to its needs, which are understood by its people. It would be foolish to destroy the administration if it is sound. On the other hand the two firms need to be run as one as soon as possible. There can be no single satisfactory answer as individual cases vary so much. Ideally, one of two situations would exist: either the new firm's systems would be perfectly suitable and entirely compatible with the buyer's, or they would be so appalling that the buyer must ride roughshod over them and install his own. Ideal situations are scarce, so some change is likely to be needed. The one guiding light is speed: if the systems are not acceptable or not understood, the acquisition is out of control.

The final point, the mutual understanding between people, will come about only if they believe they are part of the same team, are judged on the same criteria, and otherwise treated fairly and openly, being given the chance to work together and develop mutual trust.

Taxation and other liabilities

The company's solicitor and accountant should be consulted on every aspect of the deal, otherwise the chance exists that tax burdens could be increased instead of reduced, expected tax windfalls may not materialise, personal tax charges may be incurred, together with extra liabilities to suppliers, customers, staff, former staff, and so on.

It is at times like these that professional advisers really earn their fees.

Chapter 8
New Products

Most people's first thought when they consider expansion is that new products or services have to be developed. As mentioned in previous chapters, there are several avenues that should be exhausted before even a moment's thought is given to new product development (commonly referred to as NPD).

Essentially, the task in selling anything to a customer is to find out what his problems are and solve them for him. This applies whether or not the product is common or unique, brand-new or as old as the hills. In a perverse way, outside the high-technology areas, it often seems as if the more profound the consideration given to finding the true nature of the problem, the simpler and cheaper the solution. If a problem can be solved cheaply, the opportunity to produce good margins of profit is usually greater. Conversely, superficial thought frequently seems to generate complicated and expensive 'cures'. Because they are expensive they are sometimes unable to show the high margins of the cheap solution.

To make that statement is to presuppose the existence of an ascertainable cost of any problem. In many instances that is the case. A process may employ 200 people, and a new device offers to halve the labour cost. Its value to that factory is roughly the marginal cost of employing, administering and accommodating 100 people. Whatever the device itself costs to make is of little or no account to the customer, except as a possible means of driving a better bargain. His main interest, however, will be in improving his competitiveness, or his margins, or perhaps a little of each, by acquiring the device at an appropriate cost. He might even be prepared to pay more for the device than his assessable savings, in order to get the benefits of exchanging a reliable machine for unreliable people. While the costs of lost production can be quantified, some of the most important advantages of greater reliability may be intangible: a quieter life with fewer emergencies, for example.

If it is possible to do so, it is usually best to price in terms of

NEW PRODUCTS

the customer's gains from the purchase. Not only is this sound theoretically — the market must determine the price, and so on — but it makes for a more rational presentation to the customer. There are limits, of course. However much benefit a product brings, if it is quite obviously made out of three plastic spoons it will be difficult to argue for a price tag of £199.

The main benefit of this approach to pricing is that it kills off, before it is even made, the product that can never be worth the customer's while. The idea can then be returned to the drawing-board, where it can either be redesigned to a lower cost, or buried.

Some industries work on the 'cost-plus' system. Their customers pay the production cost of the item, plus an agreed margin. This obviously curtails the freedom to set prices, but firms in such industries can often make things for sale to customers who do not use that system.

Certain products make no calculable saving at all. They cost money but offer no tangible return, yet people are falling over themselves every day of the week to buy them. They include some of the artefacts held most dear in our society, the things which people most aspire to own. Gold watches, jewellery, expensive clothes: none of them tells the time better, keeps us warmer or more waterproof than cheaper counterparts, yet they are thought by most people to be highly desirable. This means that they can be sold for prices higher than is justified by their production cost, making them more profitable than their cheaper equivalents. The mystique surrounding them that makes them worth more is something that manufacturers obviously work hard to develop. It clearly applies to some extent to fairly practical items such as cars — why else is a Mercedes more expensive than a Rover? The materials and labour in each cost about the same, so the Mercedes must be more profitable. Staying with transport, it even applies to heavy trucks which one would expect to be an entirely rational purchase based on initial cost, running cost, reliability and resale value, perhaps spiced by loan or lease terms. Buyers will rationalise it in those terms, but they do seem to get a real kick out of buying an expensive Volvo or a Magirus-Deutz, but not when they buy a more lowly make.

Another factor influencing pricing decisions is the expectation of competitive reaction. This can go two ways: either price low to make the idea of competing unattractive, or price high so as to recover the investment before competition strikes, being ready to cut the price when it does. Examples exist of the latter strategy working superbly, because the competitors never did come in, so that huge profits were made.

Thus, assessing the price that the customer is prepared to pay is sometimes a matter of calculation, sometimes one of judgement, but usually involves both in varying degrees. Emphatically, it is not based solely on calculating the tangible benefits to the customer of making the purchase.

Identifying customers' problems and needs

The typical approach to NPD is to focus on the product, to try to make a 'better' widget. In the absence of any indication from the customer of what 'better' means, people have been known to pursue a merry dance around fantasy-land, usually led by a wrong-headed engineer. After months or years of earnest effort, the 'better' widget is unveiled to the customers, whose ungrateful indifference proves to be massive. Then the inquest starts, but the verdict does not always nail the real villain. How can this sort of thing happen? Right at the outset the firm decided to try to do something better, showing the correct competitive instinct. Unfortunately, it immediately took a wrong turn, by ignoring the customer, preferring instead to please its engineer. For some reason he placed engineering excellence above commercial realism — the wrong-headedness referred to — and the rest is history. Engineering excellence has its place, of course, but only when it confers benefits that customers will pay enough for.

One of the most attractive examples of doing things differently is the example of the manufacturer of a small component used on every mechanical and electrical engineering assembly line in the world. Instead of trying to make a better product, he looked at the way his customers used it, coming up with an original and highly successful approach. He looked at the whole system of how his product was made, packed, supplied to the customer, and used, quickly identifying a problem which he and his competitors were giving their customers. On arriving at the customer's assembly line, the items had to be disentangled before they could be used. This meant that for every person involved in that part of the assembly there was one person employed full time on disentangling. By making a simple change to their packaging they supplied the product in a cheap dispenser, cutting out the need for the customer to disentangle. Needless to say, the package is heavily patented, and has enabled them to take a major share of their market, at the same time charging prices higher than most of their competitors.

A list of well-known examples of looking at the customer's needs might include:

- The Andrews MacLaren baby buggy: much easier to use than the old-style pushchair
- Mothercare shops: as their slogan said, 'Everything for the Mother-to-be and her baby'
- Black & Decker 'Workmate': a portable, folding workbench for do-it-yourselfers and building tradesmen
- Services that deliver sandwiches to offices
- Firms that maintain other firms' first-aid cabinets
- Firms that charge to take away high-value scrap which they then sell.

In some, or even all of these cases, the customer probably did not articulate his need for the product or service. Nobody asked Edison for a light bulb before he invented it. This partly explains why smaller firms are usually better at innovation than their larger counterparts. In the big firm the career-conscious manager is likely to be punished more for making a mistake than he is to be rewarded for getting something right. Thus he will tend to try to reduce his uncertainty by carrying out market research into any and every proposed move. Not only does this delay things, but poorly designed market research can lead to the conclusion that a potential winner is really a dead loss. Really badly used, market research will be relied on to provide ideas for new products: people are notoriously good at complaining, but generally lack the imagination to think of solutions to their problems. Smaller firms, on the other hand, are usually more willing to back a hunch. This means that they make more mistakes, of course, for some of the subjective judgements on which products are launched make one's hair stand on end. But they also get it right some of the time.

This is not an argument against market research as such, but a plea that it be used wisely and properly. There is a definite need for entrepreneurial flair and risk-taking when new products are to be launched, qualities which the larger firm usually lacks. The small firm would be imprudent to rely on them alone, but allied to common sense, fact-gathering and analysis they can be formidable.

SUCCESSFUL EXPANSION

It may be argued that the enormous failure-rate of new products launched into the mass grocery trade, where only a handful of new products survive for a year or more, supports the need for more rigorous research and less entrepreneurial flair. To say that is to miss the point. The writer's view is that the failure rate is due to putting the producer's need first. Because the big manufacturer wants growth, he places great pressure on his staff to design and launch new products. These are often based on some research finding made by very young people in the marketing department. They are usually birds of passage, subscribing to the idea that to stay for more than two or three years in one firm is to risk becoming stale. They therefore depend upon making a quick hit and moving on, the very opposite of the long-term view needed to nurture and develop a brand name. By the time the failure of the new product has become apparent the person responsible for recommending and organising its launch may be away to a more senior post in another firm. If that is one key to the problem of new product development failure, it is one to which doing more research is no answer.

New product development budgeting

As mentioned in Chapter 6, there is a tendency in the small firm for research and development costs to run up into the stratosphere. Even the larger company which should know better is not immune from the tendency. It is therefore vital at the outset to plan a budget for cost, use of time, and completion dates for each stage. Of course, it is not easy to foresee how long problems will take to solve, or indeed to spot all the problems that will arise. But some sort of estimate, however crude, should be made. The more the project breaks unknown ground, the more conservative the budget should be; that is to say, the lower should be the forecast of benefits, and the higher should be the forecast of time involvement and costs, and the more remote the forecast completion date. Any plan is better than no plan at all, for it provides a measure against which progress, or the lack of it, can be judged. If a plan exists it may prompt the whistle to be blown on a project which is getting out of control, whereas if there were no plan perspectives would adjust themselves to accommodate variances as time went on. It is very easy for the costs of an unplanned project to run away to disastrous levels.

Budgeting the completion time, and breaking that down into target dates for completing each stage, are also important. Planning provides a control on the time that the overall project takes to finish, which might be important if there is a race to be first on the market with a new product. It also provides a prompt to review progress against timing schedules, as well as cost restrictions, at each stage of development. These periodic reviews are useful to re-plan following stages in the light of lessons learned, or even to call a halt to the whole idea. Again, there is the chance to think before possibly pouring good money after bad. Overspending on NPD is a well-known way of sinking an otherwise sound small firm. Anything that guards against it must be worth considering.

Government and other help

Nowadays smaller businesses are encouraged to apply for government help that, only a few years ago, was available to their larger counterparts only. Quite properly, the government officials responsible for handing out the cash will require a thoughtfully prepared budget for the proposal. They will check it, and have been known to suggest that it is under-costed, and they should therefore emphatically not be treated as the enemy. If they approve the proposal they can offer very substantial help: one-third of the budgeted cost is not uncommon, as a straightforward cash gift. Alternatively, they can offer up to half, but then there may be strings attached in the form of a royalty on sales.

Another form which government help can take is free or subsidised assistance for the company's design team. Under one scheme the experts of the Production Engineering Research Association (PERA) are offered free for five days' work and at a subsidised rate thereafter. The Council for Small Industries in Rural Areas (CoSIRA) employs a number of technical specialists in different fields who are heavily subsidised to help small firms develop new products. Contact points for both organisations are shown in Appendix 4.

Polytechnic and university students often have problems in finding an industrial project to count towards the qualifications for which they are studying. Some people are inclined to dismiss all students as layabouts, but as highly qualified, highly motivated, highly intelligent people, they can be hard to beat. Only their expenses need be covered, and using them can give the firm access to some very sophisticated expertise. Not only are some of the advanced students formidably effective people, but they can use superb libraries, reference facilities, and good computing, test and calibration equipment, and if they get into trouble they can call in top-class professorial talent to help out. Many firms have found students to be an excellent source of nearly free help. To get the best results from them — important because, although costs are minimal, experienced and senior staff time will be spent on briefing and liaison — the subject tutor should be approached with the proposal. He will want to help his students first and foremost, so some persuasion may be necessary to show him the true scope of the opportunity he is being offered. Once he understands how exciting it is, he will do his best to place a suitable student with the firm. It must be remembered that a student will have his own objectives for the placement, so it is important for all concerned that the project and his contribution to it are fully discussed and understood on both sides before a commitment is made.

Creative thinking

When new product ideas are to be considered, it helps to have the feeling that all likely avenues are being explored. Having only one or two possible courses of action on the shortlist can give rise to the suspicion that other, more exciting, possibilities have been overlooked. That is easily said, but how can a longer list be created?

In recent years much attention has been paid to the whole field of creative thinking. Books devoted to the subject have been written — mainly by Dr Edward de Bono, a Cambridge academic. Cruelly paraphrased, the main thrust of the experts' ideas is that normally our thinking will proceed along straight lines, making obvious connections and coming up with no very original ideas. The really great ideas, the ones that seem so obvious and so naturally right, are rarely reached by plodding forward along straight lines. That does not mean that they are not connected to the earlier ideas. On the contrary, once thought of, their connection to the former position can be seen very clearly; which is why everyone wonders how such an obvious idea could remain hidden for so long.

It is more difficult to describe the processs than to cite an example. A lovely one occurred during the petrol shortage in the 1970s. Over most of Europe, motorists were allowed to buy only a maximum amount of petrol at each purchase. In the UK it was usually four gallons. As a result, people visited filling stations far more often to buy the odd gallon to keep their tanks full. The outcome of keeping the tank of every car in the country brim-full was a worsening of the shortage at the pumps, the very opposite of the desired effect. In one small country, famous for its original ways of looking at things, they had no such problem. In the Republic of Ireland they enforced a minimum purchase: anyone taking a smaller quantity had to pay the full price of the statutory minimum purchase. Result? Few queues at the pumps and, more important, the precious national stock of petrol was available to those who needed it, rather than sitting in the tanks of occasional motorists who did not.

The rightness of the idea was immediately obvious, yet in Britain we had not worked it out for ourselves. Instead, we thought along straight lines: shortage = rationing = maximum purchase. The conclusion was obvious and its outcome damaging. The Irish came up with an apparently scatterbrained idea that was perfectly right for the conditions, and brought about exactly the result that their government wished.

For some rare people that kind of sideways thinking comes naturally. For that reason they tend to gravitate to jobs where the accent is on new ideas, and the best of them can charge highly for their talent. Many experts maintain that less elevated mortals can cultivate the gift themselves, which experience has borne out many times. There are two main techniques that can be usefully employed in NPD. One is to list all the attributes of the present product — weight, height, smell, brightness, colourfulness, and so on. Then to think of what it would be like if each of those attributes were to be changed, usually by exaggerating it and by diminishing it. If the technique is applied to an ordinary pot of marmalade, the list might look like this:

Attribute	Extra/less	Other changes	Possible appeal
Height	Higher/shorter	—	Elegant/homely, tall one packs better on shelves.
Width	Fatter/slimmer	Short and fat looks like marmalade pot for table?	Homely/elegant, see above. No need for separate marmalade jar — larder to table pack.

105

SUCCESSFUL EXPANSION

Attribute	Extra/less	Other changes	Possible appeal
Volume	More/cheaper	—	High value/pensioner, single-person pack.
Cylindrical pot	Globular/cubic	—	Homely, distinctive/gaunt. See 'Height'.
Glass package	Pottery/metal	Rigid plastic, plastic 'sausage', cardboard	Quality/cheaper.
Colour	Richer/paler	—	More nourishing, heartier/elegant, distinguished.
Consistency	Thicker/thinner	Coarser	Coarse, thick = nourishing, 'home-made'.
Sweetness	Sweeter/bitter	—	Mass-market/'elegant' (cf dry sherry).
Label colour	Colourful/plainer	—	Homely, rich/'elegant'.
Metal cap	Plastic/paper	Gingham trim	Gingham = homely, paper = 'home-made'.
Fruit	—	Try others than orange, lemon, grapefruit, lime	Novel (= 'smart')?

From this simple exercise a number of possible new marmalade products can emerge. We might investigate further three from the list which seem to have possibilities:

Rich, sweet, coarse-cut marmalade in a globe-shaped or dumpy pot, possibly opaque, with a gingham-trimmed lid and 'busy', colourful label which can be peeled off easily. Its appeal would be 'home-made', rich, nourishing; the interesting pot would catch the eye and be suitable for use on the table, with or without its label, thus saving the sticky job of topping-up the marmalade dish.

A pale, bitter, fine-cut product sold in a tall jar, possibly of glass but maybe of slip-cast pottery, with an elegant, simple label probably fired on to the pot in the kiln. Its appeal would be to those seeking elegance, part of which may have associations with its low-calorie content. Possible variants and sister-products may be 'interesting' varieties of non-citrus preserves — quince, mulberry, or others.

As possible outside chances, smaller versions of the above to serve as sampling purchases, gifts, purchases by single persons and pensioners. Very small versions as two-serving portions for caterers.

That example proceeded along traditional straight lines. It created a number of new ideas of the product and resulted in two defensible product ideas that might bear further investigation. Regrettably, they are also rather obvious.

To think really creatively, it helps to use the technique called 'brainstorming'. This involves deliberately switching off all critical faculties and letting the mind freewheel. It is best done in small groups — three to six people seem to work best — with one member of the group jotting down the ideas while joining in. Some people advocate using a tape-recorder or a shorthand-writer to keep the record, but the sense of someone overhearing seems to inhibit the proceedings. Brainstorming involves dropping inhibitions, especially those about looking foolish. One member of the group introduces the theme to be developed — it might be a shoe polish firm trying to find a better way of protecting leather shoes from salty slush in winter. By association of ideas the thoughts sparked off within the group might run in a sequence like this:

Waterproof polish — greasy polish — spray-on plastic coating that can be peeled off — polish containing chemicals that neutralise salt's attack — spats — giant wellington overboots — lightweight, foldaway, zip-up nylon overboots — throw-away plastic bags, elastic-necked and styled like spats, in different colours — etc.

In this list the company has a number of product ideas with potential to overcome the defined problem as well as other difficulties associated with footwear. Some are impractical: anything that changed the composition of salt would probably do even worse things to leather, and the giant wellington boots could be ungainly and difficult to walk in. However, they were not attacked at the time by the group, as that would have stemmed the flow and could have caused someone to switch off with hurt feelings. Only after the session is over, and 15 minutes is usually long enough if the mental juices are flowing, do the members of the group criticise. Even then they do it constructively — what materials could be used for the giant overboots to make them light and elegant as well as waterproof? Often there will emerge a clear winner. In this case money could perhaps be put on the last two in the list, and possibly number three. (Due apologies to anyone who has already marketed these ideas — the author made up the list on the spur of the moment to answer a particular irritation of his own, as well as to provide an example.)

Because people need to be relaxed to do this well, it can be a good idea to create an informal setting in which it can take place. Drinks at the end of a long day and a light, jokey atmosphere often work well. If people spend a lot of time laughing during the session, that does not matter, indeed it can be a good sign. It can be a mistake to include the persistent comedian who tries to get a laugh out of everything, for he can reduce the whole effort to meaninglessness. But witty people are those who easily see unusual ideas and contribute well. There are no general rules for whom to include, except that they must obviously have the capacity to accept the idea of behaving rather strangely for a few minutes in a good cause.

Developing a list of ideas is one thing, judging their manufacturing practicability and appeal to customers is another. That can only be tried out by more conventional methods. It is important to recognise these limitations of brainstorming, but they in no way diminish its usefulness in uncovering new ideas. Even so, when the commercial tests give those ideas the thumbs-up, there may be sound reasons for killing the idea or at least pending it, for instance, because it is an awkward fit with the present range.

Other people's ideas

Firms can expand using ideas that they themselves have not developed. As a method it carries the obvious risk that the inventor may decide to take his idea away, but in some industries and for many companies it can be the answer to the problem of NPD. After all, if someone has already invented it, why try to repeat the process?

FRANCHISING

Taking on a franchise is the easiest, quickest, and in many cases the most foolproof route. In some fields, catering for example, it is a fast-growing area. But it does suffer from the twin drawbacks of the franchise possibly being not as well tested and developed as the propaganda suggests, and the more or less complete dependence on someone else's continued success for the survival of one's own firm.

DISTRIBUTORSHIP

Franchising will suit some companies, but others will look at their strengths and weaknesses, and identify products that they could sell alongside their own, if only they could lay hands on supplies. This can place the firm in a very strong position in times when there is more capacity than there are orders. Under those conditions the man who can get the orders is in control. Manufacturers will be attracted most by a distributor who offers, in no particular order:

- ☐ Proven sales ability
- ☐ Complementary product range
- ☐ Net extra sales
- ☐ Integrity
- ☐ Appropriate after-sales service
- ☐ Ability to collect debts on time
- ☐ Financial stability.

Some industries have their own special requirements, but the above list holds more or less generally. The selling firm also has its own requirements of a supplier, which are in some ways the mirror-image of the above. If the supplier is from overseas, it will be further complicated by the usual cross-frontier questions, mainly to do with exchange rates, payments systems, and exchange controls.

JOINT VENTURE

Circumstances can arise where a distributorship is not acceptable to either side. The maker wants a hand in selling and the seller wants a stronger hold on the maker, let us say. In this instance it may be right to float a joint venture, a jointly owned and directed third company with allegiances in both directions but a separate life of its own. As in any commercial relationship, it is advisable to take early legal and organisational advice (which are not the same things) on the implications. Just as it is possible to set up an arrangement which cannot be executed because the legal risks are too great, arrangements can be made in which the safeguards are so solid that the business cannot move. Hence the mention of the organisational aspect, which is especially important where joint ventures are concerned.

Patents

As soon as somebody invents something, his first thought is usually to patent it. While that may be wise, it will also be costly, but even more costly will be the expense of suing anyone who infringes the patent, which can easily run to over £10,000. If the action succeeds, the other side should pay, but they might simply go into liquidation or the action might fail. Either way, the costs of the legal system may mean that a patent is, in any practical sense, indefensible. All it might do is to frighten off some possible copyists, or encourage a larger firm to buy the idea from the inventor as a quick and easy way of adding it to their range.

That may be too gloomy a view to take, but it is put forward to balance the euphoria that often accompanies the development of a patentable idea. The company's best course of action is to talk over with a patent agent the protection offered by patents, registered designs, and copyright, and listen to his advice about the best course of action in its particular position.

While on the subject of patent agents, it is worth mentioning them as a means of obtaining introductions to inventors of new products. At least one major international company mails regularly to them, suggesting that their inventor clients with patented products may wish to sell out. If they find it worthwhile, so might a smaller firm.

Chapter 9
Finance

All the different types of finance available to a company fall clearly into two categories, short term (usually an overdraft facility, which gives the bank the right to repayment in full on demand) or long term (with agreed monthly instalments over a period of years). The distinction is crucial as they fulfil quite different roles, yet people are often confused by the fact that they are measured in the same pound units. Despite that, they are very different.

To illustrate the danger of confusing them, consider the plight of the five-man firm that borrowed £80,000 short term to buy premises, planning to pay it off with expected earnings from a couple of plum contracts it had been promised. The contract did not materialise, damaging their profitability and cash flow. That harmed their reputation at the bank, whose unease was compounded by a government credit squeeze which threatened the company's market and caused the bank to reduce or call in altogether its riskier overdrafts. Having no prospect of reducing the overdraft, the company was forced into liquidation. The main cause of failure was the short-term financing of what should be seen as a long-term purchase. Cash flow and profit problems did not help, of course, but they were not the primary reasons for failure. Had the firm taken out a 20-year loan, all the bank could have called for in any one year would have been the repayments, £13,000 at most, instead of the whole £80,000. As a result, they might have scraped through. Or, if they had eventually failed, it would not have been because of a foolhardy piece of financing.

Thus it is important to finance longer-term needs — buildings, equipment, machinery, vehicles, and so forth — by longer-term finance. Short-term funding is appropriate to only short-term needs, covered by the blanket term 'working capital', meaning the wherewithal to meet the day-to-day bills, instalments on loans, wages, general running expenses and tax liabilities. Equally, it is wasteful to borrow a sum on long-term loan if it is needed only for a short time to cover working capital needs.

It is also important to consider how easy it is to borrow money for different purposes. Many new starters in business make the mistake of committing their savings to buy equipment and premises and then find that the bank is reluctant to lend working capital. The motive seems to be the entirely understandable desire to own one's workshop and tools, but money for fixed assets is fairly easily come by, either from the bank or, more expensively, from finance companies. It is often wiser for the new starter to borrow for long-term needs and hold his own cash back for working capital.

If the expanding business finds itself with a disproportionate amount of its funding coming from short-term sources, it should consider restructuring its present financing as part of any proposal to borrow more. Occasionally a firm with plenty of collateral for its borrowing may find that the bank has allowed it to buy equipment on overdraft, perhaps not wishing to trouble its busy owners with ideas of converting part of the overdraft into a term loan. That is meant helpfully, but it will be the very opposite if a vital new borrowing proposal goes up to the bank's area office who take one look at the lopsided balance sheet and send it straight back. As a general rule, banks are happy if every pound of borrowing is matched by a pound of owner's investment, but guarantees covering further borrowing can make them more flexible.

The main sources of funds are:

— Equity: risk investment by the owners, including directors' loans
— Loan: banks, finance companies
— Credit: suppliers.

Any company's aim must be to increase the owner's share of the financing by producing earnings which can be retained from the cash flow. This reduces its financing costs and makes it more of a master in its own house. The growing company does the same thing but for different reasons. Its expansion needs to be financed — more equipment and materials to buy, more overheads incurred, more money owed by customers. Thus, increasing the owner's share of the business via retained earnings enables it to ask the bank to match the rise in the owner's funds with bigger lending.

Similarly, suppliers are often willing to grant credit to growing businesses on the assumption that helping them to grow by giving them longer credit earns goodwill that may come in handy later. It is risky to see this for anything more than it is, a way of holding down the overdraft which, though convenient, cannot be relied on forever, or to finance long-term projects.

Evaluating capital needs

Forecasting the need for money to buy new equipment is relatively simple. The timing of the purchase is known and its cost is shown in price-lists and quotations. Even so, there is no need to rush off to the bank to raise a loan. A supplier might offer credit terms. Even if they are not offered at first they might be available, perhaps at higher cost. The extra cost could be worthwhile if for some reason bank finance is to be avoided, or it might even be cheaper finance than the bank can offer. This is especially likely if the manufacturer of the equipment is overseas, where government export aid or lower interest rates may enable a good deal to be offered.

Working capital requirements take a little more effort to assess. They vary as money moves out of the business to pay its bills, and in from its customers, all out of phase with one another. Cash flow forecasts will reveal the working capital implications of proposed policies, showing when and to what extent deficiencies are likely to occur. The bank can be approached to cover these temporary shortages, most probably by way of an overdraft facility. Indeed, these days a bank will expect cash flow forecasts to accompany any request for borrowing.

Well before the decision is taken to invest in a piece of equipment it is wise to assess the return it will bring. If this is done for all the proposed investments in the business it might show up an area where uneconomic investment is being considered. Clearly, a new piece of equipment must be expected to earn a return sufficient to cover its own depreciation, interest on the loan to buy it (or interest forgone if it is bought with cash in hand), and its running costs. Over and above that the firm may set itself a target for a return on its investments. In Chapter 7, when a takeover was being considered, methods of assessing and comparing investments were discussed. They can also be applied to the proposed investments in different parts of the firm. For instance, it might be seen that buying a company car produces little benefit over and above the leasing method, whereas outright purchase of a machine gives a far better return.

Thus the company can formulate financing policies for different parts of the business which will have the effect of raising the average return earned on the total investment. It is possible, and very easy, to become mesmerised by these issues. In no way should they dominate or alone decide the company's course of action. They usually serve as useful additional sidelights on the decision, which it would be foolish to ignore.

Likewise taxation: some businessmen become obsessed with the idea of avoiding tax (avoidance is legal, evasion not), so that they seem to run their businesses to minimise their tax bill rather than as tools for earning money by satisfying customers' needs. Certainly the tax reliefs should be taken, and the decision as to what is to be purchased and when should be informed by tax considerations, but tax should not be the sole deciding factor.

Grants may be available which will also affect calculations of the capital requirement. The principal ones are available in the government Assisted Areas. They are Regional Development Grants at 15 to 22 per cent of the cost of new buildings and new machines, claimed retrospectively as of right and available to manufacturers; and Regional Selective Assistance, a discretionary grant which is negotiated on the basis of the applicant's need and his likely future contribution to the economy. Local authorities, tourist boards, and industrial quangos may also have grants available, but in practically every case it is necessary to apply in advance of starting the project, otherwise the applicant risks disqualification.

Grants, too, should not be viewed as ends in themselves. Otherwise the firm risks finding itself with some free money, but in premises that are at the wrong end of the country for its customers. Despite all the propaganda about grants for business, they are mainly one-off gifts to offset part, but only a part, of the cost of a purchase, and not a crock of gold which they can be made to sound like. Just as with tax reliefs, they are very useful but rarely justify radical changes of course.

From time to time, governments come up with short-lived grants and subsidies for particular activities. Recent examples include the £15-a-week subsidy for employing young people, and the one-third grant for buying computer-controlled machine tools. To keep in touch with this changing scene (which sometimes foxes the civil servants) it is worth ensuring that the firm is on the mailing-lists of the appropriate public bodies. The Small Firms Service in particular makes a point of mailing to its clients details of any new grants or benefits which are announced.

Sources of finance

Several sources have already been mentioned in passing, but a more formal list could be useful. Only the most popular providers of finance are mentioned here, rather than every possible source. This is designed to save readers from wasting time in pursuing many fruitless enquiries.

BANKS
The clearing banks are the first line of finance for almost every business. It is right that this should be so, for they offer an unrivalled range of services. They are not, however, identical. Policies from the top will colour local managers' decisions, which is one good reason for shopping around and keeping in touch with more than one bank. For the size of business represented by this book's readership, it does not make sense to run accounts at more than one bank. But some expanding firms regularly meet managers of other banks, and even supply them with a copy of the monthly reports prepared for their management, which they also send to their own bank manager. The relationship which this cultivates might, they hope, stand them in good stead one day, and they are not running risks with their secrets for good bankers are discreet.

The banks to which an ambitious firm makes advances will probably comprise only members of the 'Big Four'. As large firms, they can offer the specialist expertise that the company is likely to need, and they do undeniably advertise a wider range of services than their smaller brethren. For example, 20-year loans for buying a factory are advertised by the Big Four banks only, and none of the smaller houses. The really methodical businessman will get from each bank a list of services offered, and compare them. It may show up one bank's weakness in a vital area — export finance, for instance.

The main loans offered are well-known: short term (usually by way of overdraft), medium-term loans of up to seven years, and long-term loans of seven to 20 years. In addition there are available specialised methods of financing exports, and introductions to other members of the same group: a merchant bank, a finance house, an insurance subsidiary, and so on. These introductions can be useful, but the borrower is well advised to

SUCCESSFUL EXPANSION

pursue enquiries outside the banking group if he is to get the best deal, even if that means only that his bank's approach is sharpened by the knowledge that others are in the race too.

Banks will always look first at the viability of the enterprise which seeks to borrow from them, but at some point the question of collateral for the loan will be raised. That might take the form of a debenture on a limited company's assets or directors' guarantees, or personal guarantees from partners or sole traders. It is vital that the firm pledges as little of this collateral as it can get away with, keeping back as much as possible for the inevitable day when it goes back for more. Unlimited or general guarantees are to be avoided: if £10,000 is being borrowed, a £10,000 guarantee should be given, and so on.

Many expanding small firms have exhausted their borrowing capacity and, despite marketing opportunities, dare not grow further because the necessary working capital is not available due to the lack of further collateral. The government Loan Guarantee Scheme (LGS) was introduced partly to overcome this problem. Under LGS, the bank lends all that the small, viable firm with a sound project needs, the bank taking the risk on 20 per cent and the LGS guaranteeing up to 80 per cent, to a maximum of £75,000. There is a premium to the LGS fund of 3 per cent of the element which it covers, over and above the bank's interest rate. While nobody likes paying extra for money, many small firms have found LGS to be a lifeline in their struggle to expand and remain solvent.

When negotiating with anyone, it is important not to be unrealistic, and this goes for banks too. The interest which banks charge is normally quoted as fixed or floating, and as being so many percentage points over base rate. The smallest firm will usually pay 4 per cent over base, and the very largest around 1 per cent. The rate agreed may vary with different loans, and indeed it should, partly reflecting as it does the degree of risk to which the bank feels exposed. An expanding small business buying a workshop, where the bank's risk is covered by a mortgage on a good industrial property and the rest by LGS, might borrow at as little as 2 or 2½ percentage points over base. Simultaneously, its overdraft might be charged at 3 or 4 per cent over.

Other ways of reducing the costs of borrowing are to refuse to pay 'arrangement fees', or at least to have them reduced, and to enquire about local authority and EEC subsidies towards interest rates. At the time of writing the EEC's European Investment Bank is offering funds through the clearing banks and others at only a couple of percentage points over base rate, and where steelworks or coalmines are being closed other subsidies may be available.

While on the subject of banks, there is one piece of information which the businessman should know about his branch manager, his 'discretionary limit'. That is the amount he can lend without asking permission from area office. By choosing to deal with too small a branch the business could incur delays and unaccountable refusals to lend, simply because the decisions were really being taken elsewhere, and not at the local branch.

INSURANCE COMPANIES
Useful for a long-term project like buying premises, insurance companies can offer competitive loans.

MERCHANT BANKS
Once the firm has reached a certain size it may consider selling shares to raise money. Its natural resistance to diluting its independence may be strengthened by the knowledge that an astute investor will buy shares only if he has a very good idea of when, how, and to whom he will sell them. Before coming to an agreement with such an investor the firm may wish to consider the full implications very carefully, and perhaps seek to limit the investor's freedom, for example by insisting that shares for sale must be offered to the directors or their nominees before they are sold elsewhere. In any case, the firm will want to ensure that an outsider does not hold a controlling interest, and for that reason may agree to sell only a 20 to 25 per cent stake; keeping the proportion sold so low has another benefit — if more shares eventually have to be sold, the outsiders' stake can still be kept below 50 per cent.

Probably the best-known merchant bank is ICFC Ltd, part of a group formed by the clearing banks and the Bank of England to provide merchant banking services to the smaller firm. In addition to equity investments, ICFC is prepared to make straightforward loans with no shareholding.

For those firms destined for the stratosphere, a merchant bank can help with placing shares on the Unlisted Securities Market and eventually on the Stock Exchange itself.

SUCCESSFUL EXPANSION

FINANCE HOUSES AND LEASING COMPANIES
These firms usually offer both hire purchase agreements and leases. The difference lies in two main areas: with hire purchase the tax reliefs go to the hirer, but to the leasing company for leased goods; and hire purchased goods become the property of the hirer at the end of the agreement, while leased goods usually do not, though there are exceptions. Thus, while the two terms are often used interchangeably, they have very different meanings.

In addition, many of these companies offer long-term funds for such purposes as buying and equipping premises.

PRIVATE INVESTORS
This breed was nearly extinct until changes in the tax rules encouraged people to make equity investment in small firms. Now individuals paying the top rates of tax can invest in businesses at a cost after tax relief of less than half of the amount invested. Investment institutions have seen the opportunity that this represents and are offering those investors the chance to spread their risks by lending their money to a range of small firms. At the time of writing, it represents a good deal of money looking for a home.

SUPPLIERS AND CUSTOMERS
If suppliers allow 30 days' credit it is unnecessarily virtuous to pay them in seven. At the same time, few ever expect to get paid that quickly. Equally, the customer who delays payment for three months is likely to get a bad reputation and even have credit facilities withdrawn, so it is wise for the company to look after its suppliers to an appropriate extent, remembering that this can vary with the toughness of trading conditions. The important fact is that supplier credit is the cheapest form of finance any company can ever have.

As well as being a customer, a firm is itself also a supplier. It is not for nothing that the very large firms who take an age to pay their bills are often the best chasers of money owed to them: perhaps there is a lesson here for the smaller firm striving to get big. In its role as a supplier the company could do worse than examine and question the basic assumptions in its industry about payment of bills. It should also beware of assuming that any industry or class of customers with which it starts to deal absolutely must have its normal conventions observed. In some cases it may be possible to introduce a deposit with the order, or a proportion payable on delivery, instead of assuming that everyone expects a conventional credit account. Firms that fall into this trap are often industrial suppliers who begin to deal with the public. Industry generally expects credit accounts, it is true, but even there exceptions exist, whereas the public expects to pay cash on delivery or installation. The difference that this can make to cash flow scarcely needs mentioning, so it deserves more than a moment's thought to seek some way of introducing it that seems credible to customers.

Relationships with lenders

Lenders deserve respect, right from the earliest point in the relationship. The case for the lending should be put to them in the form in which they expect to receive it, and they should be given enough time for digestion and consideration before a meeting takes place. They should be taken fully into the borrower's confidence. Confidences will be respected, and bankers are adult enough to know that not everything is 100 per cent perfect in every firm. If the warts are not described as well as the beauty-spots, the lender will be searching for them, because he knows they exist. He needs to know whether they are harmless or, if not, under treatment to control them. The borrower who openly admits and discusses them will gain increased respect. This should not be taken to excess, of course. The main purpose of the approach is to build confidence, not to confess inadequacies. Suggestions by lenders should be taken seriously; the banker may know little about the borrower's industry, but he does know about banking, and the breadth of his experience across many industries makes him a man worth listening to. Questioning of any aspect of the firm and its policies should be met with candid, truthful but positive explanations. If the borrower has anything to hide he should remember that there are onerous penalties for obtaining money under false pretences. In those circumstances he is best employed sorting out the mess into a state where he can speak truthfully of it, show the steps being taken to sort it out, and the likely speed with which recovery will take place.

If breaking his word is unforgivable in a banker, the same goes for a borrower. Commitments, once given, should be kept to. Accounting reports which have been promised should be delivered on time. Less under the borrower's control are the actual events he forecast, his cash inflows and outflows.

Variations are allowable, even expected, but the bank also expects that the borrower will spot them, and report to them on the implications before events deviate too widely from the plan. This implies that the borrower is in control of his business, as discussed in Chapter 4. Quite apart from the respect for the banker's position which it also implies, it means that the borrower may have the time calmly to negotiate different arrangements if necessary. The lender will look askance at any customer who does not realise that he is in trouble until the bank tells him. He also dislikes duress. 'You've got to lend me enough for the week's wages,' said at ten minutes to one on a Thursday really is asking for the answer, 'Why must I? The bank requires you to submit a proper lending proposal and to make an appointment with me to discuss it.' Bless them, most bank managers would not actually say it, but they would want to.

Limited companies

Most firms begin their lives as sole traders or partnerships. At some point, growth will force them to consider the possibility of 'going limited'. The decision will probably be based on one or more of the following:

— The need to issue shares to raise finance
— Taxation
— The desire to reduce exposure of personal assets to commercial risks.

Limited companies' profits are taxed on a scale between 30 and 50 per cent, to be reduced to 35 per cent by 1987. Individuals are not taxed on their first slice of income, then pay tax progressively, starting at 30 per cent and rising to 60. The 1984 Budget has diluted the incentive to sole traders and partnerships to reduce their overall tax bill by becoming a limited company. The firm in a business open to large, unpredictable, or long-term risks — a construction contractor, for instance, whose buildings could start to show cracks ten years later — could wish to be limited so that if the worst happened only the firm would go to the wall. His only personal loss, apart from his reputation and livelihood, would be his investment plus any of the company's debts that he might have guaranteed. Had he been a sole trader all his personal, as well as business, assets could have been sold to satisfy a successful claim.

These areas, and all others connected with taxation and

liabilities, can be highly complex and can vary with the industry and the type of firm. The only way to handle them successfully is to take the advice of competent professionals in private practice, solicitors or accountants as the case may be.

Chapter 10
Production

The idea of expanding the business seems to inspire in some people a reflex action of looking at shiny new premises or sending off for glossy brochures about the latest equipment. Except in the most extreme cases of decrepitude, that can be a trifle premature: the first task is to get as much as possible out of existing resources. More output from present resources, incurring no more overhead than is currently being paid for, is a recipe for maximum marginal profit. It therefore deserves serious attention.

The place to start is to assess exactly where the firm is at present, seeing what resources it has and the use it is putting them to. To make a simple analysis of capacity, all that is needed is to take each machine, or each department, or whatever division of the production side of the business makes sense, and state its capacity. Often the best way is to follow typical products right through the entire process from receipt of raw materials or sub-assemblies to the despatch bay, including transport if the firm operates its own. This will tell the owner what theoretical maximum output could be achieved at each stage of production if everything ran smoothly and at 100 per cent efficiency for a whole working year. The year is probably the best unit of time to use, as at a later stage it helps the decision whether or not holidays should be for fixed close-downs, or staggered across the work-force as a whole, and other seasonal questions.

A plant can run only at the speed of its slowest process. That will be identified by the analysis, making it easy to see which area is holding back progress. As mentioned earlier, spotting the problem virtually defines the solution. By overcoming the drag in one department or process the bottle-neck is shifted elsewhere, to the second slowest on the list, where action needs to be concentrated if more production/still is called for.

Although the justification for this approach may seem to be self-evident, every consultant who has looked for any time at a production question can cite examples where clients have been saved from costly 'obvious' solutions by their consultant's more analytical approach. A couple of examples: a manufacturer was saved from having to double his premises costs to get a bigger materials storage area, by storing in racks instead of on the ground and simultaneously discontinuing the stocking of infrequently used items (the local wholesale stockist agreed to hold stocks for him on good terms, in return for a sole-supplier agreement); a servicing firm got out of its costly workshops by converting to mobiles which carry out the work on the customer's premises instead. This achieved a marketing coup, as well as attracting better staff (via the perk of a company van available for private use) and keeping them longer, which improved quality.

The latter example was inspired by two further factors. One was the hard questioning of function which accompanied the analysis of capacities. It is surprising just how much woolly thinking can grow up in a firm about exactly why it goes about its work in the way it does. This trio of questions ought to be written on every manager's wall, not least on that of the production manager:

Why do we do this, and in this way?
Need it be done at all?
Is there a better way of getting the desired result?

The other factor which inspired the second example was an examination of where the firm's profits are really made. Often companies do or make things for themselves that they could buy in more cheaply. That can make sense if it is a conscious decision based on some sound arguments, such as security of information or the recovery of overheads; but those two reasons have vastly different implications for the growing company. Issues of security must be viewed as truly important, but what may rightly have started as an exercise in filling some spare capacity must not be allowed to continue occupying that capacity when resources are scarce. The item or process can be contracted out, freeing space for a better money-earner. Too often the reason for the decision to make in-house is lost in the mists of time and it becomes assumed that it should continue for no better reason than custom and usage.

Another way of putting this argument is the idea of concentrating all the firm's effort on what it is good at, the area where its earning-power is greatest. There can be no better example than Marks & Spencer, whose strength is in retailing, which is what they keep to. They must have been tempted from time to time to venture into making things. For a time they would probably be among the best, but a captive customer of that size would be a terrible temptation for their manufacturing arm to become complacent. It is far better to induce manufacturers to keep themselves up to date by dangling the carrot of large orders for the most competitive, and to stick to keeping shop better than anyone else. This idea has implications well beyond the production area of course, as discussed in Chapter 3, but just as the broad strategic thrust of the company is under constant review, so are the important operational questions. Neither is more important than the other, but each is vital in its own way.

Having defined the firm's theoretical maximum capacity, it is instructive and often very humbling to compare what is currently being achieved. This comparison will undoubtedly show some strange variations in the proportion of capacity being occupied. At all costs there must be resistance to the temptation to brand the low performers 'lazy'. It might be the explanation, but there are others which are far more likely, such as variations in:

— Reliability of machines
— Availability of materials
— Materials quality
— Scrap and re-work
— Operator skill levels
— Length of production runs
— Managerial effectiveness in different departments
— Effectiveness of recording work done.

A really comprehensive list could go on for pages, but this will serve to illustrate that it should be approached in the first instance as a management problem. The chances are that men standing around idly are unoccupied through no fault of their own, yet the lazy or ineffective manager will persist in blaming everyone else but himself for that state of affairs. The effective manager concerns himself with identifying the real, underlying cause, and gets to work on curing it, even if it does involve an element of self-criticism.

The outcome of all this investigation will be a clear picture of where gains could be made. It is but a short step to attach costs, where indeed they would be incurred, to each option.

The benefits of each can also be quantified, so it is now fairly straightforward to assess the most profitable step or series of steps. At some time it will be necessary for most growing firms to extend their premises or move altogether, but if the pattern which has been outlined is followed, they will ensure that this costly and disruptive step is taken only when it really is the right thing to do. Before that stage is reached it will be necessary to see the various operating options open to the firm — overtime, contracting out, night-shifts, more staff, better equipment etc — are compared on a common basis so that foolish assumptions are exposed and decisions are taken in such a way as to make the best use of the firm's resources. This can only improve profit.

Efficient production

The factory can be run at something like maximum efficiency if it performs only one process non-stop. Few businesses can run like that, but control of a variety makes an important contribution to the efficiency of the production function. In addition to matters discussed earlier in this chapter, there are two approaches to institute:

- ☐ Reducing any variety that is not necessary
- ☐ Keeping under control whatever variety is necessary.

Variety can build up in the growing firm at an alarming pace. New products are launched, adding to the size of the price-list, to the number of warehouse locations needed and to the number of change-overs necessary in the factory. They also necessitate their own stock of spare parts, the addition of new raw material stocks, and the number of different items over which to exercise stock control. It helps if new products can be designed as far as possible as derivatives of existing lines, subject to all-important marketing factors, of course. Designers can also contribute by using common components and processes as far as possible. They will probably do this only if management announces it as part of the design brief, and continues to emphasise its importance at every opportunity.

The owner casting an eye over the range of products his company makes could do worse than calculate for each one the benefits of continuing with it. The task is simple: to calculate the income from each product and rank the results in descending order; then to work out the gross profit from each (income, less direct materials, less direct labour and any other cost uniquely attributable to it), and rank those in descending order. The ideal product is one which generates most income and most gross profit, and such products will obviously be retained. Those making a good profit will also qualify to be continued. In both instances it would be interesting to see if sales volume can be increased. The products that perform poorly on both dimensions should not be automatically abandoned, for they might be immature and have yet to find their feet, or be important flagship products, or make a small but useful contribution to general overheads. If there is no justification of this kind for their retention they can be critically examined to see if costs could be reduced or sales volume, and/or prices, increased. If it seems unlikely that any such alteration will rehabilitate them, they must be considered for discontinuation. The owner who takes these sorts of decision in an analytical way stands to gain not only in productive efficiency, but perhaps in sales volume as well. The concentration of marketing effort, aided by the clearer identity produced by a less diffuse range, has been known to more than replace the sales lost.

The jobbing company, making to customers' specifications, may be able to benefit by looking at the families of products it is called upon to make, to see if there is an opportunity to standardise any elements. The 'package deal' colour printers, typically offering 5000 A4 leaflets for under £200, are an excellent example of this in action. By standardising on the A4 paper size, and ignoring the opportunities for customers to select non-standard shapes and sizes, they have grouped together a number of orders to give the benefits of long-run prices on quite small quantities. The low cost is more than enough to persuade the customer to give up his freedom and to accept standardisation.

Quality and its control

'Quality' is a widely used word, yet it is by itself virtually meaningless. It is therefore much misused and misunderstood, yet the concept is of vital importance to business. In its industrial and commercial sense it has meaning only in relation to the purpose or function of the product. Indeed, it has two meanings: the fitness of the product's specification and design for its purpose, and the degree to which the end product conforms to those specifications. The former has already been touched upon, so it is the latter which will now be discussed.

Failure to achieve acceptable quality standards has well known consequences: valuable work is scrapped, customers have costly breakdowns which are expensive and disruptive to deal with, warranty claims exceed budget, reputation and customers are lost, and so on. But exceeding acceptable quality standards is also expensive. A truck maker may dream of launching a marketing drive based on the 50 miles per gallon heavy lorry, but the huge increase in production cost will make management think again. Although the customer might put that at or near the top of his list of desirable attributes of the product, he would be unlikely to pay treble the price to attain it. Hence the emphasis on an 'acceptable' quality level. Different policies will give different meanings to the word 'acceptable': acceptable quality for an aircraft is (or ought to be) different from that for a box of matches.

Closely linked to the notion of quality is that of reliability. However fit for its purpose a product is, it must continue to perform its function well enough for long enough to satisfy the customer. That does not mean forever, just enough to make the customer feel that, taking all the circumstances into account, the product has performed well. Again, a quality car is expected to last longer and to break down less frequently than a hack. At between six and ten times the price, so it should. This attitude is attacked by the ecological lobby. That in itself provides marketing opportunities and perhaps explains in part the resurgence of the technically obsolete but long-lasting Morris Minor — an opportunity which one entrepreneur has been quick to exploit with excellent replicas. In the conventional wisdom, the car is over-specified, labour-intensive in production, and plain old-fashioned. But the replicas sell.

If there are general rules for minimising the risk of failure, they include design and production simplicity, building in safety margins, and using well trodden production and design concepts. It also helps if standard parts are used which the customer can replace from local stockists rather than from the manufacturer only: there is no point in making life difficult when a breakdown does occur. It also helps if the risk of early breakdowns is minimised by running in the product before delivery. If more manufacturers took the trouble to do this, it would eliminate a high proportion of the early failures that do such damage to reputations.

Manufacturing tolerances are frequently vital to the maintenance of quality and attendant reliability. It is possible, but costly, to inspect every single item the factory makes. Where very small numbers are involved and high quality is mandatory, that might be the best course. However, once any volume of production is established it becomes for all practical purposes impossible. In such circumstances it is best to look for help to the principles of statistical sampling and apply them to the quality control task. The basic idea is to select only a few items periodically and test those for conformity to standards. If they fall inside acceptable limits, production is allowed to continue. If not, they will fall into either a warning zone, alerting the inspector to make further checks because tolerances may be moving beyond the acceptable, or an action zone where performance is not acceptable and machines must be reset. This is a well-documented subject which will repay further reading.

In a small firm it is normal for the operative to be self-censoring on quality matters. If he does substandard work he takes remedial action. As companies grow it is often thought necessary to install quality control inspectors. Before this step is taken, the possible consequences should be carefully considered. It may be necessary for the appointment to be made in order to ensure that management has adequate information on quality matters, but this benefit can easily be outweighed by other effects. The production staff must not be allowed to think that the new man relieves them of the need to bother about quality. They must not get into the frame of mind that the inspector is an enemy to be hoodwinked whenever possible into accepting substandard work. Thus, the inspector's terms of reference need to be clearly spelled out and emphasis placed on the individual's continuing responsibility for the quality of his own output.

Systems

As the business expands the old methods of keeping on top of the job in hand are no longer enough. Once upon a time the boss knew a job was slipping behind because he was himself working on it. He came in for a couple of evenings after supper and caught up. When he is no longer personally involved on the shop-floor, and when more jobs are being done concurrently, he has a problem. He has complexity to deal with and is out of direct touch. The only way he can manage is to be sure that good systems are in place and are sufficiently accurate and timely to perform two functions:

- ☐ Alerting staff to problems
- ☐ Supplying information to enable the effects of the various options to be assessed.

This requires great changes in recording from the days when the boss knew what was going on because he was directly involved, or later when he could poke his head out of the office door and shout for a progress report. To start with, control charts will appear on office walls showing the scheduling of particular jobs and progress against the schedule, and loadings in each department as a proportion of capacities. From those master documents other planning and control tools will spring: schedules of orders on suppliers, stock records of raw material items, staff time-cards, job-cards, despatch records, and purchase requisitions.

Purchasing

As time passes and the company grows, purchasing develops from an occasional matter handled by the owner to a routine handled by a clerk who may know little or nothing of what he or she is dealing with. All that distinguishes one product from another in the purchase records are a flag denoting its importance, decided by calculating the cost of running out, the minimum and maximum stock quantities, and the all-important unique identity code for the item. Some person in a senior position will negotiate terms, and it is up to the clerk to see that the agreed terms are kept to and that stocks are maintained. At some distant point in the company's progress it will become desirable for a full-time buyer to be recruited, responsible for the record-keeping function and purchase negotiations, but with a wider brief to improve relationships with suppliers and to ensure that the firm is aware of, and known to, all suppliers who are likely to be of use to it. He also plays a role in helping production schedules to be created, agreeing the payment of invoices after quality checking of goods received, assisting designers to cost new products, and trying to foresee shortages of, or price increases in, essential supplies. A really good buyer can save his company much trouble and cost, perhaps in some unusual ways such as negotiating quality controls with suppliers that will cut out the need for inspecting goods received.

A buyer has an orderly mind. He is therefore a good person

to put in charge of physical stock control. Remarkable things happen when an open store of materials is closed off and the issuing of stock placed under one person charged with answering for shortages. People start to buy their home needs, such as paint, hacksaw blades, solder, glass paper, buttons, or whatever, from the shops. If the firm has expanded without controlling the movement of stock it will probably find this a lucrative way of cutting costs. The same goes for stationery; how many office workers ever buy pencils? The staff who pocket things are rarely downright dishonest — they might take a ball-pen, but they would never help themselves to 50p out of petty cash. Depriving them of ready access to these odds and ends may save money, but the costs of doing so can be considerable. To begin with, someone will have to undertake the job of looking after the issues, which takes their time. They will have to do periodic stock-takes and reconciliations to prove that they are not walking off with the goods themselves, which takes more time. The staff may sulk about the implied criticism of their honesty and exaggerate the length of time it takes to get essential supplies from the issuer. The savings may be far less than the cost, so these arrangements should be made only if absolutely necessary.

Safety

The law requires that employers provide safe working conditions, and that employees work in a safe manner. The penalties for infractions can, quite rightly, be heavy. The owner owes it to himself and his people to ensure that they complete their working lives in his firm intact. There is no foolproof formula for success, but there are one or two things that can be done to minimise risk.

Some people recoil from the idea of inviting the inspector from the Health and Safety Executive to visit their premises to give his advice. The inspector can give more authoritative advice than anyone else, and is the obvious person to ask. Moreover, if his recommendations are observed, he is likely to be far more understanding if an accident ever does occur in the future. This is not to suggest that he will be corrupted by a cup of tea and a biscuit, but that an accident at a relatively unknown firm will perhaps be investigated with more suspicion than in one he already knows to be doing its best.

All staff should be impressed with the need to work safely.

Safety instruction should be organised for new recruits, and especially for the young. Having seen less of life and work, they are always at risk of allowing their high spirits to overrule their sketchy understanding of just how dangerous work places can be. Notice boards should carry supplies of blank safety hazard report forms, so that staff can easily and promptly report the loose stair-carpet, the jamming door, the rickety table under the photocopier. They should be addressed to the senior manager responsible for safety who has the right to cut across all company procedures if necessary to get safety hazards put right. He, too, will be responsible for organising the much-derided fire practice and all other safety matters.

The reason why fire practices and other safety matters are so lightly viewed by many staff can only be put down to a failure of understanding and imagination. The fact is that most people killed by fire die as a result of the smoke, not the heat, and very little material needs to burn to fill a room with dense smoke. Yet people do not realise it. Even relatively modest machines like photocopiers, franking machines and power hand-tools, have their hazards. Many people concerned with safety are convinced that the only way to get safety taken seriously is to develop a few graphic and ghoulish illustrations of the result of ignoring it. The bony end of a lamb chop can represent a finger, to touch the end of a woodworking machine, for example. Gory photographs, in colour, taken in casualty departments and eye hospitals can also help. It is not a pleasant approach, but neither are the possible results if the risks are not communicated.

Needless to say, maintenance plays a part in safety as well as in economical working. Certain work has to be carried out on a particular frequency, laid down by statutory authorities, insurers or equipment suppliers. The small business usually relies on operators to keep their machines up to scratch, but there are general areas that are the business of nobody in particular. Constant vigilance on the part of senior managers and awareness among employees are the best safeguards here.

Premises

When it becomes clear that the inevitable move really can be put off no longer, decisions have to be taken about the firm's new premises. Rightly, production people will have a say in their selection. They will want the location to be right for suppliers and staff. Sales people will want premises that represent the firm well to customers as well as being accessible to them. The financial people will want the best of all worlds, as usual: lowest initial cost, lowest maintenance cost, and least transport cost from suppliers and to customers. That raises the question of the character and appearance of the building: should it be brand new and look futuristic, or do the looks not matter as long as the price is low; or should it be traditional, dependable and settled-looking? The building from which it operates says a lot about the firm to staff, suppliers, and customers, so it is important. The best staff, for example, are unlikely to apply for jobs to a firm that looks as if it is run by skinflints with no care for people.

In the end, the importance of location is usually decided by customers, suppliers, or skills. It depends on the industry. Leather tanners tended to settle where there was plenty of water, livestock and oak trees, their raw materials. The footwear industry tended to settle where its suppliers, the tanners, were. Makers of packaging tend to settle where their customers are — it is so costly to ship empties around. According to studies, few firms move very far because of government incentives. If they are moving anyway and another few miles means a 15 per cent grant towards the new building and equipment, it might be worth it. Alternatively, values on the wrong side of the boundary line might be so depressed that a bargain can be had there.

Appendix 1
Statistics in Management

In a young firm's early days, most of what is to be done can be decided by the knowledge and intuition of the owner. Relying on that system when the firm has outgrown it is one of the many routes to commercial disaster. At some stage it becomes desirable to introduce some formal analysis of the firm's activities as an aid to more scientific and logical routes to taking decisions.

This is not to decry the value of intuitive decision-taking. It involves using the most sophisticated computer known to mankind, the human brain, and putting it to work with inadequate data. In such circumstances, that it should come up with any answer at all is some sort of miracle, but that it should have worked well so often throughout history is even more remarkable. This extraordinary power of the brain should be kept for the time when the facts run out, not to avoid bothering to know them. Statistical methods can help to organise facts into a shape with meaning, informing the brain so as better to secure the launching pad from which imagination can take off.

There are three main statistical techniques which can help small firms:

Probability and distribution
Regression
Correlation.

It is not the function of this book to try to teach these techniques. They are not excessively complicated to learn, and when aided by a computer their operation becomes merely a press-button matter. The reader is urged to attend a short course or obtain a book on the subject. A good example is *Statistical Methods in Management* by Tom Cass, Cassell, 1969.

This may sound like a recipe for yet more hard work. Some people do find mathematics a little challenging at first, but computers overcome that problem entirely, and even rank innumerates have been known to develop a grasp quite quickly. Everyone can understand and appreciate the significance of these techniques when they put them to work, especially when the results are produced in graphic form. Amateur statistics, on the other hand, may be misleading because the figures have not been sufficiently manipulated to reduce error, or more laborious than is necessary because sampling theories were not understood.

Probability

Life is littered with events which seem to crop up repeatedly but unpredictably. If the event is the failure of particular machine parts under stress, it

SUCCESSFUL EXPANSION

is possible almost to eliminate the risk altogether, but that is usually expensive. It involves over-specifying, extensive bench testing and 100 per cent inspection. It is far more cost effective to predict the rate of future failure from past experience, using probability techniques, and to advise replacement at an appropriate point during routine maintenance. Other applications include:

— Estimating how many customers place orders for different numbers of items from the range, as a guide to promotional policy
— Forecasting how many customers will switch from a competitor's product, based on a small survey
— Assessing whether or not a small sample is likely to represent a whole batch.

It is obviously very useful to know whether or not a sample is representative, be it of customer behaviour, invoicing errors, production mistakes, product reliability, or whatever. Hence the importance of probability.

Probability becomes an even more useful tool when it is combined with the idea of distribution. How often, and when, things go wrong (or right); how often, and when, events take a particular course, and so on, can be charted against probability. The result enables a management decision to be made about acceptable levels of risk. How much better than guesswork or intuition! Some further applications might be:

— Setting quality-control standards and tests of a few samples to replace 100 per cent inspection
— Deciding what nominal weight to fill bottles to in order to observe legal requirements about short measure
— The minimum size of service fleet needed to deal with customer calls, consistent with a satisfactory level of service
— The rate at which a faster but less accurate manufacturing method will cause customer problems, so that savings can be compared with customer complaint costs
— Estimating customers' waiting time at different levels of shop-staffing, and how often someone will be kept waiting more than a certain time.

This type of analysis helps to take the heat out of the relationship between production staff and sales people. Both can see that a specific service level has been chosen because it is the most beneficial. Neither expects 100 per cent perfection or 100 per cent failure, and the idea that a particular level has been selected, rather than happening through carelessness, helps the salesman to see the reasons why. There are obviously other uses and benefits, but that is just one which is far removed from most people's idea of a statistician's contribution to a firm.

Regression

Everyone is familiar with the sort of simple graph that charts two dependent factors against each other. They might be shoe size and height, engine size and fuel consumption, or industrial injuries and safety training. If the different points on the graph can be connected by a straight line, no further statistical work is called for: that single line perfectly expresses all of the points on the graph. Things are rarely that simple, because the points on the graph are usually dotted all over the place. Even if they tend to cluster around an imaginary line, it is possible to draw that line in a number of different places and still have it fitting fairly closely to the points. This is where linear regression comes in. Estimating the line that would best fit the points of the graph is usually unreliable, involving the risk that decisions will be taken on false assumptions. Linear regression is the process that calculates the line that will best fit the points on the graph.

Multiple regression enables the effects of several factors to be considered at once. For instance, a plant may be working at maximum output, and the manager wants to be sure that the most profitable mix of products is being produced, given that each one places different demands on individual departments whose resources are finite. Multiple regression will enable him to calculate this very clearly. It is applicable to many other areas of business. Even within the factory, when the question of product mix is being considered, its use is not limited to a situation of maximum output; it can be used to calculate the most profitable mix of production at any given level of output.

Correlation

If the regression line is only the best fit that can be obtained to the points on a graph, some idea of how closely it fits the points can be useful. Correlation measures the degree to which the line does represent all the points, enabling its reliability to be assessed. A correlation coefficient of 1.0 means it is a perfect fit, and can therefore be relied upon for any reading in the range dealt with. A coefficient of 0.2, on the other hand, means it is only 20 per cent representative and that little reliance should therefore be placed on it.

Appendix 2
Financial Planning

Three simple but powerful techniques can be of great use to the growing firm. All look to the future, providing a blueprint against which progress can be checked:

> Profit and loss budgeting
> Break-even analysis
> Cash flow forecasting.

In addition, simple costing systems will be looked at.

Profit and loss budgeting

The profit and loss budget usually deals with the year as a whole, although it can usefully be broken down into (say) monthly or quarterly sections if desired. A typical P & L budget looks like this:

	\multicolumn{4}{c}{Month}			\multicolumn{3}{c}{Year to Date}	
	Actual	%	Budget £	%	Actual	%	Budget £	%
Sales			20,000	100			240,000	100
Cost of Sales								
Materials			5,000				60,000	
Labour			6,700	11,700	58		80,000	140,000	58
Gross Margin				8,300	42			100,000	42
Overheads								
Rent			670				8,000	
Rates			80				1,000	
Wages			1,250				15,000	
Drawings			800				10,000	
Phone			20				200	
Electricity			60				800	
Vehicles			80				1,000	
Advertising			80				1,000	
Stationery			20				200	
Post			20				200	
Repairs			10				100	
Publications			10				100	
Insurance			20				200	
Sundries			20				200	
Professional fees			60				800	
Bank charges			20				200	
Depreciation			80				1,000	
				3,300	17			40,000	17
Trading Profit				5,000	25			60,000	25
Interest				1,000	5			12,000	5
Net Profit before Tax				4,000	20			48,000	20

The *sales* figure includes everything that is expected to be invoiced, irrespective of whether or not it will be paid for in the period covered by the budget.

Cost of Sales is a slightly misleading term. It really means 'cost of goods sold', and includes only those materials and labour costs directly involved in producing the goods or supplying the service. Any labour costs incurred elsewhere — for instance, in selling or clerical functions — does not appear under this heading. They do appear, but under 'General Overheads'. There is a reason for separating the business's fixed costs which do not vary from the costs which go up and down with the amount of business done. It will become apparent later in this appendix.

The figure for *Gross Margin* is arrived at by simple subtraction of Cost of Sales from Sales.

Overheads are all the other costs of the business excepting the costs of finance. Generally speaking, they do not vary very much, however much (or little) business the firm does. Over a long period they will increase as the firm grows; more rent will be paid, for example. But over a shorter term they are more or less fixed.

Arriving at the *Trading Profit* is another simple subtraction, this time of the total of Overheads from Gross Margin. This is done before financial costs are counted. The reason for this is to separate two quite distinct issues. The profit that the firm makes from trading is something that it needs to know about, irrespective of interest charges. Of course, interest has to be paid, but if it is not separated out the beneficial effect of a reduction in interest rates could conceal a dangerous decline in trading margin. The presentation shown avoids this possibility.

Net Profit before Tax is another simple subtraction, this time of interest cost from Trading Profit. The figure shown is unlikely to be wholly taxed, as tax reliefs usually have to be applied to it.

If one thing is certain, it is that the actual results will not be identical to the budget. Thus the columns for reporting what actually happen serve a useful purpose. They help to highlight the areas where the variances are serious, as a focus for management action. This process is greatly helped by the percentages, which convert everything back to a common base, once more enabling different effects to be identified. An increase in volume might show higher profits, but this should not be allowed to obscure any loss of percentage margin, which is sometimes an early warning of a collapse into discounting.

Break-even analysis

As the name suggests, the idea is to identify the level of sales at which the firm 'breaks even', that is, it earns enough to cover its costs but not to show a profit. This is where the separation of Fixed Costs from Variable Costs comes in. The following definitions need to be absorbed:

Fixed Costs. The costs that the firm will incur even if it does very little business indeed. Most of them are under the heading of Overheads, but financing costs should be added in. When deciding what category a cost should fall into, one need not be too dogmatic.

Variable Costs. Those costs which go up and down with increases and

SUCCESSFUL EXPANSION

falls in sales. For practical purposes this means materials used in production, and labour costs of the actual production process.

The result is usually displayed graphically:

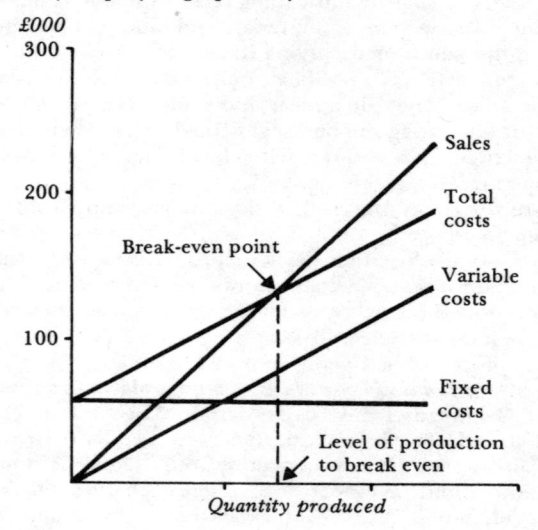

[Graph: axes labelled £000 (vertical, 0–300) and Quantity produced (horizontal). Lines labelled Sales, Total costs, Variable costs, Fixed costs. Break-even point marked where Sales and Total costs lines cross, with dashed line down to Level of production to break even.]

From this, the firm can see:

At what quantity of production it breaks even; this must be its minimum target

How much profit or loss it will make at different levels of production

What margin of safety the firm has: that is, how far its planned sales are above the break-even point. Put differently, that is the extent by which sales can fall below plan before the firm makes a loss.

Cash flow forecasting

The function of this activity is quite different from those of the calculations above. They dealt with aspects of profit, ignoring whether or not the suppliers had been paid or the customer had paid their bills. A very simple business will have no need to forecast cash flow: customers pay bills in cash, and all costs are paid in cash. Thus the profit and loss account describes the flow of cash.

In the sort of firm with which this book deals, the picture is more complex. At the end of the year, some of the bills will be unpaid, and some of the customers will owe money for goods sold. During the year the movement of cash out to suppliers and in from customers will go up and down, so that sometimes the bank account will be full of cash and at others it will be overdrawn.

The importance of cash is easy to describe: without it, the business fails. If enough cash is not available to pay the bills as they fall due, the creditors will probably take legal action to seize assets which can be sold to pay their bills. Thus the control of cash in the business is of vital

FINANCIAL PLANNING

importance. It especially needs to be applied in two contexts:

— When the annual plans are being prepared, to identify the times when cash will be short, so that bank overdraft facilities can be negotiated well in advance of the need
— When a change of policy or an opportunist purchase or sale is being contemplated, to see what effect it will have on cash.

The latter is particularly important. Many a firm has been unable to resist the chance to buy a bargain lot of stock, or new equipment at a low price, and then run out of cash and gone to the wall.

The task of monitoring cash flows, and of looking at the effect of different policies on the likely cash position is greatly simplified by the microcomputer. Even some home computers can now use the so-called 'spread sheet' programs that are set up for this kind of exercise. Instead of having to do a lot of laborious arithmetic to arrive at different scenarios, the change of a few figures at the beginning of the run will ripple through automatically to recalculate the whole forecast.

Shortly we shall take the profit and loss budget shown on page 136 and make some assumptions to assemble a cash flow forecast. But first, a brief and simplified example to show the method:

		Jan £	Feb £	Mar £	Apr £
Cash received					
From sales	(a)	500	1,000	2,000	2,500
Less:					
Cash paid out					
Rent		200	–	–	200
Wages		500	500	500	500
Purchases of stock		200	400	600	600
Other costs		100	100	100	100
Total paid out	(b)	1,000	1,000	1,200	1,400
Net cash in month (a–b)		(500)	–	800	1,100
Cumulative cash		(500)	(500)	300	1,400

(brackets = negative)

Starting with no cash, the firm expects to take in cash (a) and to pay out cash (b) in each month. Subtracting (b) from (a) shows the cash situation at the end of the month. All that now needs to be done is to work out running totals for the month-end figures to show the cumulative cash. That last figure is, in effect, a forecast of the bank balance, sometimes in credit, sometimes overdrawn. In this case the firm needs to provide for a £500 shortfall during January and February, after which it will go into the black. This is a vital planning document for the firm and for the bank, who can see that this request for an overdraft has been arrived at in a disciplined way rather than, as so many are, being guessed at.

Two points to bear in mind when writing cash flow forecasts, both related to the fact that they reflect only movements of *cash*, are:

When the sales invoice is issued, or when the supplier's invoice arrives,

SUCCESSFUL EXPANSION

	Nov £	Dec £	Jan £	Feb £	Mar £	Apr £
Sales forecast	20,000	10,000	10,000	15,000	20,000	20,000
VAT received	3,000	1,500	1,500	2,250	3,000	3,000
Total	23,000	11,500	11,500	17,250	23,000	23,000

Cash Flow Forecast, January to December

	Jan	Feb	Mar	Apr
Cash received				
Cash sales	2,875	4,312	5,750	5,750
Debtors	17,250	8,625	8,625	12,938
Other: loan			10,000	
Total cash in (a)	20,125	12,937	24,375	18,688
Cash paid out				
Materials	2,875	4,312	5,750	5,750
Rent	2,000	–	–	2,000
Rates	–	500	–	–
Wages	7,916	7,916	7,916	7,916
Drawings	833	833	833	833
Phone	–	60	–	–
Electricity	–	250	–	–
Vehicles	92	81	230	92
Advertising	92	92	104	92
Stationery	58	–	–	58
Post	10	20	20	20
Repairs	10	10	10	10
Publications	8	8	8	8
Insurance	–	200	–	–
Sundries	20	20	20	20
Professional fees	–	–	800	–
Bank interest	1,000	1,000	1,150	1,100
VAT	–	–	–	4,813
Tax	–	–	–	–
Capital items	–	–	10,150	–
Loan repayments	1,100	1,100	1,300	1,300
Total paid out (b)	16,014	16,402	28,291	24,012
Net cash (a–b)	4,111	(3,465)	(3,916)	(5,324)
Opening bank balance	–	4,111	646	(3,270)
Closing bank balance	4,111	646	(3,270)	(8,594)

VAT calculation	1st qtr £	2nd qtr £
Outputs	6,750	10,500
Inputs	1,937	2,715
Payments	4,813	7,785

FINANCIAL PLANNING

	May £	Jun £	Jul £	Aug £	Sep £	Oct £	Nov £	Dec £
	25,000	25,000	20,000	10,000	25,000	25,000	30,000	15,000
	3,750	3,750	3,000	1,500	3,750	3,750	4,500	2,250
	28,750	28,750	23,000	11,500	28,750	28,750	34,500	17,250
	7,188	7,188	5,750	2,875	7,188	7,188	8,625	4,312
	17,250	17,250	21,563	21,563	17,250	8,625	21,563	21,563
	24,438	24,438	27,313	24,438	24,438	15,813	30,188	25,875
	7,188	7,188	5,750	2,875	7,188	7,188	8,625	4,312
	–	–	2,000	–	–	2,000	–	–
	–	–	–	500	–	–	–	–
	7,916	7,916	7,916	7,916	7,916	7,916	7,916	7,924
	833	833	833	833	833	833	833	837
	40	–	–	50	–	–	50	–
	150	–	–	200	–	–	200	–
	81	92	81	92	81	92	81	58
	92	104	92	92	115	115	115	46
	–	–	58	–	–	58	–	–
	20	20	20	10	20	20	20	10
	10	10	10	–	10	10	10	–
	8	8	8	8	8	8	8	12
	–	–	–	–	–	–	–	–
	20	20	20	–	20	20	20	–
	–	–	–	–	–	–	–	–
	1,100	1,150	1,100	1,100	1,150	1,100	1,100	1,150
	–	–	7,785	–	–	5,566	–	–
	–	–	–	–	–	–	–	–
	–	–	–	–	2,000	–	–	–
	1,300	1,300	1,300	1,300	1,300	1,300	1,300	1,300
	18,758	18,641	26,973	14,976	20,641	26,226	20,278	15,649
	5,680	5,797	340	9,462	3,797	(10,413)	9,910	10,226
	(8,594)	(2,914)	2,883	3,223	12,685	16,482	6,069	15,979
	(2,914)	2,883	3,223	12,685	16,482	6,069	15,979	26,205

	3rd qtr £			4th qtr £	
	8,250			10,500	
	2,684			2,700	
	5,566			7,800	

141

SUCCESSFUL EXPANSION

is immaterial; what is shown is when they are likely to be *paid*.

The cash flow forecast will relate closely to the profit and loss budget, except for depreciation, capital equipment purchases and VAT. Depreciation is not a movement of cash, and capital purchases and VAT do not appear on the profit and loss budget.

Cash flow forecasts are also useful in 'What if?' planning. What if sales are 20 per cent less than budget because prices have to be cut? The reader could try working this through. *(Answer:* the bank account will be in overdraft rising to £600 in January and £800 in February, falling to £400 in March and creeping back into £200 credit in April.) Or what if the customers don't pay as planned, but hang on to their money for another month? *(Answer:* the overdraft keeps on climbing — £1,000, £1,500, £1,700, £2,300.)

Now for the full-blown cash flow forecast based on the profit and loss budget shown on page 136. First, some assumptions must be made:

— The firm starts this forecast with no cash in the bank.
  25 per cent of sales are cash, 75 per cent are paying two months after the invoice is issued.
— Materials are bought in the month before they are turned into goods and sold, and paid for a month after purchase. Thus, they are paid for in the month when the goods are sold.
— Rent is paid quarterly in advance.

Even though we are dealing with a company that has prospects of making a sound profit, its requirements for cash vary greatly from month to month. On the basis of this forecast it will need an overdraft facility getting on for £9,000 at the end of April. This is in spite of the new equipment, valued at £10,000 + VAT, which is to arrive in March, being financed by a separate loan. The business already has other loans, of course. Yet by the end of the year it expects to have £26,000 in hand.

In practice, the firm would probably negotiate a facility for a £10,000 or £12,000 overdraft to make sure that they were on the safe side. Although the cash position at the end of April is forecast as almost a £9,000 shortfall, if the suppliers were to be paid at the start of the month and the customers were all to pay at the end, the overdraft could rise as high as £27,000, so a little leeway is desirable, as well as strict control over when payments are received and made.

Appendix 3
Business and the Law

A huge volume of law affecting business has built up over the years. No businessman can operate safely without at least a sketchy idea of how it can or could affect him. Most of what is written here applies only to England and Wales; Scotland has its own system.

Business names and constitution

If someone operates a business as a *sole trader* he is personally responsible for the debts of the business, and the business profits are his wages. If he uses his own name, without adornment, there is no need for him to observe any regulations concerning business names. Thus, if John Brown is a butcher, trading as plain John Brown or J Brown, he is in the clear.

If he wishes to call his firm Brown's the Butcher, or some other name which is not exactly his own, there is one simple set of regulations which he must observe. Until January 1982 he would have been required to register the name at a central registry, now abolished. Now he should do three things:

- ☐ Display prominently on the business premises in a place to which suppliers and customers have access, a notice saying 'Particulars of ownership of (trading name) as required by Section 29 of the Companies Act 1981. Full names of proprietors: (insert names). Addresses within Great Britain at which documents can be served on the business: (insert addresses).'
- ☐ Disclose in writing this information immediately it is asked for by anyone with whom anything is discussed or done in the course of the business.
- ☐ Disclose on letterheads, invoices, statements, receipts and demands for payment, the names and addresses of the owners of the firm.

A *partnership* is much the same as a sole trader, with the vital exception that each partner is individually responsible for the debts of the business as a whole. Thus, in a two-partner firm, if one decamps with all the money, the one left behind is responsible for all the debts, not just half.

A *limited company* is very different. In law it is a separate person both from its owners and its shareholders (who can, of course, be the same people). Thus a limited company that crashes is responsible for its own debts, and the owners/directors can walk away from the wreckage, their personal fortunes intact apart from any investment that they may have made in the firm. The only exception is any liability which they have personally guaranteed: if insufficient funds are raised by the sale of the firm's assets, these creditors can call on the guarantors to pay up. Typically, only the banks or other institutional lenders are secured in this way. Most firms start life as sole traders or partnerships, and take the decision to transfer to limited company status based on the following factors:

Taxation. At a particular stage of profitability, corporation tax may cost less than personal tax. There are other tax situations in favour and against.

Risk. A firm which incurs long-term liability for its products may wish to reduce the personal impact on the owner of a disastrous claim. An example might be a pharmaceutical company, or a builder, where a fault might lie dormant for years and then result in a catastrophic award for damages. Insurance may be appropriate here.

Finance. An investor might be reluctant to make a loan, but be prepared to buy shares.

A limited company may use a trading name other than its own, in which case the same disclosure rules apply as to the sole trader or partnership.

The law

There are two distinct branches: civil and criminal law. The criminal law is laid down by Parliamentary statute and the police will be interested in anyone who breaks it. Civil law has never been defined by Parliament but has grown up over the centuries as a result of judges' decisions about particular cases. Anyone with a grievance against someone else who appears to be breaking the criminal law may ask the police to step in. If, on the other hand, there is a grievance but no law is laid down to cover it, the plaintiff may ask the courts to settle the issue under the civil law. The judge will be guided by the innumerable decisions of his predecessors to establish the rights of each party, and will then make up his mind on the basis of how they were exercised or infringed in the case before him.

There are, inevitably, grey areas between the civil and criminal codes. If a customer does not pay his bill, that is a civil matter, and the supplier will usually sue to get settlement. If it can be shown that the customer never meant to pay, it might be a criminal offence in one of the categories close to stealing.

For all practical purposes the businessman needs to know about any areas of criminal law that affect him in his particular business, plus two branches of the civil law.

CRIMINAL LAW

The main areas covering most firms are:

Trade descriptions: not misleading about goods or services. Consult County Council or Metropolitan Authority Trading Standards Department.

Employment law: take specialist advice.

Work-place law: health and safety, various equipment regulations, fire regulations, building regulations, Factories Acts and regulations about record-keeping; specialist advice is needed, or help from

Health and Safety Executive.

Consumer credit: if credit is given to members of the public, take advice from a solicitor.

Doorstep selling: customer has right to 'cooling off' period; can also apply to some showroom sales. Consult solicitor.

Exemption clauses: it is a criminal offence to try to deprive customers of legal rights although sales to business may be subject to 'reasonable' exemptions. See free leaflet: 'A Trader's Guide — Law Relating to Supply of Goods and Services', from Small Firms Centres.

Motor vehicles: most aspects are too well known to need elaboration here. Beware special regulations for heavy goods vehicle operation and drivers' hours. Check with Department of Transport.

Specialised industries: many industries have a particular body of regulations which must be observed.

Wages Councils: it is an offence to pay less than Wages Council rates. About 30 industries, including shops, clothing factories and caterers, are covered.

Planning consent: it can be an offence to change the nature, times or scale of the activity conducted on premises; check with solicitor, surveyor, or local authority Planning Department.

Exchange controls: operated by many countries; in UK currently lax but could be tightened. Check with bank.

Prohibited exports: some technological products may be exported only by special permission; advice from Department of Trade and Industry or British Overseas Trade Board.

Subcontractors: Income Tax Deduction Exemption Certificates may apply to some self-employed subcontractors, especially in the construction industry. Check with Inland Revenue.

Price and wage controls: no maxima apply at present but they could be reintroduced.

Import controls: some products or materials may not be imported, others may, but are subject to control. Check with Department of Trade and Industry, Ministry of Agriculture, Fisheries and Food, or British Overseas Trade Board.

Credit controls: usually affect HP sales; used by governments as an economic control, and impose a minimum deposit.

Insurance: public liability and employer's liability insurances are required by law.

CIVIL LAW

Law of contract

A contract is made when three factors are present:

Offer: someone has something to sell.
Acceptance: someone else wants to buy it.
Consideration: it is agreed that something will change hands, usually (but not always) money.

If the law is to be used, it is best to avoid the courts unless the matter in dispute is of such compelling importance that there is no alternative. Many is the firm that has entered on litigation, the only result of which has been the enrichment of the legal profession. One exception to this general rule is when the small claims procedure of the county court is used. Here, claims for up to £500 can be settled by arbitration without even reaching the court, with no need for legal representation and at low cost.

The main reasons for legal disputes over contracts are either that one party has not understood fully the implications of what he has agreed to, or that the agreement was so sketchy that each party took away widely differing views of what had been agreed. The latter point does not mean that everything that is agreed upon must invariably be the subject of a bulky, written contract. Rather, that a few notes in the form of Heads of Agreement should be drawn up and agreed on both sides. Sensible people can usually sort out the problems that arise in a continuing relationship, even though the written agreement did not cover them in detail. If they are at loggerheads, the odds are that the relationship is, in reality, already over and that some pretext is being sought by one side to end the arrangement.

The fact that an agreement is not confirmed in writing makes it no less binding, of course. The written word simply makes it easier to prove what was agreed.

Any contract obviously incorporates the terms which it states, '£100 per ton', '7½ per cent off list price', 'delivery by April 21', and so on. But in addition there are implied terms which, though not spelled out, also apply to every contract made. The main ones are:

The seller has the right to sell the goods.
The goods comply with the description given.
The goods are of 'merchantable quality' and fit for the use that the customer specified: they will do what could reasonably be expected of them. The only exceptions are where the seller pointed out the fault, or the buyer scrutinised the goods in such a way that he could reasonably be expected to have seen it.
The bulk that is delivered corresponds with the sample shown.

The above implied terms are some of the 'conditions' of the contract; that is, they are so important that if they are breached the injured party is entitled to his money back plus damages. 'Warranties' are the other terms, less important, where a breach entitles the plaintiff to damages only.

Tort

There are various torts, of which the main one affecting the honest business is that of negligence. Here again, there can be overlaps with the criminal law. It may be negligent of the firm to leave a loose carpet unattended to: someone tripping over it may successfully sue for damages under the civil law, while there is probably also an offence under the Health and Safety at Work legislation. The other civil wrongs are:

Nuisance: noise, smells, obstructions etc
Defamation: damaging the character of another person
Conversion: selling stolen goods, even if innocently bought
Trespass
Passing-off: faking another's product
False imprisonment: wrongly detaining people.

Terms and conditions of sale and purchase

For very sound reasons, big companies sell their goods on terms favourable to themselves. The terms were part of the contract because, appearing in brochures, on quotations and order forms, they formed part of the 'offer'. That they were printed in light grey ink, in small type and written in special legalese does not excuse the buyer from reading and understanding them. Likewise, when a big company buys something it places the order on an official form which also carries terms and conditions of purchase. That constitutes part of the 'acceptance'. None of these terms could have been unilaterally inserted retrospectively, so their timing is vital. At some point in its growth, the small business will want to emulate the big boys by giving itself valuable legal cover. Most people review the buying and selling terms of several big firms whose expertise they respect, and rough out a draft that suits their own company. Their solicitor then looks it through and corrects it ready for publication.

Where two sets of terms and conditions are competing, one from buyer and one from seller, the rule of thumb is that the last one in sticks. Hence the charade of a quotation on A's terms, an order on B's terms, acknowledgement of order on A's terms, that goes on. In that example, A would probably win.

When discussing these matters with the company solicitor the question of 'reservation of title' should be raised. This is originally an American concept which is gradually being adopted in the UK. In essence, it can give protection against the customer who goes into liquidation. In the normal course of events, everything sold to the customer is the liquidator's to dispose of, irrespective of whether it has been paid for. If title in (that is, ownership of) the goods has been reserved until the goods are paid for, it may be possible to get one's goods back from the liquidator.

Appendix 4
Useful Addresses and Information

Some of the schemes mentioned are temporary, any may be withdrawn at any time, others are probably permanent. It is worth asking around for information on a specific area of interest in case a new scheme becomes available.

Management and technical advice and information

Council for Small Industries in Rural Areas (CoSIRA)
Local offices in phone book, or HQ at 141 Castle Street, Salisbury, Wiltshire SP1 3TP; 0722 336255

Federation of Microsystems Centres
Help with selecting microcomputers, and familiarisation
Microsystems Administration Unit
National Computing Centre Ltd, Oxford Road, Manchester M1 7ED; 061-228 6333

Highlands and Islands Development Board
Bridge House, Bank Street, Inverness; 0463 34171

Local Enterprise Agencies or Boards
Enquire of local authority or public library.

Northern Ireland Development Agency
100 Belfast Road, Holywood, County Down; 02317 4232

Local Enterprise Development Unit
Lamont House, Purdy's Lane, Newtownbreda, Belfast BT8 4AR; 0232 691031

Production Engineering Research Association (PERA)
Melton Mowbray, Leicestershire LE13 OPB; 0664 64133

Research Associations, Trade and Industry Associations, Government Research Establishments

Scottish Development Agency
120 Bothwell Street, Glasgow G2 7JP; 041-248 2700

Small Firms Service of Department of Trade and Industry
Dial 100, ask for freefone 2444.

Technology Advisory Point
Department of Industry, Ebury Bridge House, 2-18 Ebury Bridge Road, London SW1W 8QD; 01-730 5144

USEFUL ADDRESSES AND INFORMATION

University, Polytechnic and College Business Schools and Small Firms Centres

Welsh Development Agency
Treforest Industrial Estate, Pontypridd, Mid Glamorgan CF37 5UT; Treforest 2666
Mid Wales Development (formerly Development Board for Rural Wales)
Ladywell House, Newtown, Powys; 0686 26965

Financial help from government

A wide range of government assistance is outlined in *Guide to Industrial Support,* published with *British Business,* from *Department of Trade and Industry,* Floor 11, Millbank Tower, London SW1 4QU; 01-211 6088, 6188 or 6177.

Biotechnology help: up to 100 per cent grants. *Department of Industry, Biotechnology Unit,* Laboratory of the Government Chemist, Stamford Street, London SE1 9NQ; 01-928 7900 ext 601 or 628.

British Technology Group: venture capital for small firms, joint ventures to finance projects; *Information Division, British Technology Group,* 101 Newington Causeway, London SE1 6BU; 01-403 6666.

Computer-Aided Design and Test Equipment: One-third grant for computer hardware and software purchase or lease; *Department of Industry, Electronic Applications Division,* Room 308, 29 Bressenden Place, London SW1E 5DT; 01-213 7404.

Computer-Aided Design/Manufacture: up to 100 per cent of feasibility study costs; *Department of Industry,* MEE 2 Branch, Room 401, Ashdown House, 123 Victoria Street, London SW1E 6RB; 01-212 5789.

Council for Small Industries in Rural Areas (CoSIRA): 141 Castle Street, Salisbury, Wiltshire SP1 3TP; 0722 336255: loan packages in conjunction with banks.

Energy Survey Scheme: up to 100 per cent of consultant's fees for energy-saving study; *Energy Conservation Division, Department of Energy,* Thames House South, Millbank, London SW1P 4QJ.

European Coal and Steel Community: fixed asset loans only in steel and coal closure areas, interest rate possibly reduced by 3 per cent. Barclays Bank, National Westminster Bank, Co-op Bank, ICFC Ltd or *Department of Trade and Industry* as for *European Investment Bank.*

European Investment Bank: loans for up to eight years for up to 50 per cent of fixed assets purchases; Barclays Bank, National Westminster Bank, Midland Bank, ICFC Ltd, or *Department of Trade and Industry,* Room 225, Kings Gate House, 66-74 Victoria Street, London SW1E 6SJ; 01-212 0814.

Industrial Robots: grants for feasibility study and application work; *Department of Industry,* MEE 2 Branch, Room 420, Ashdown House, 123 Victoria Street, London SW1E 6RB; 01-212 0724.

SUCCESSFUL EXPANSION

Loan Guarantee Scheme: major banks and ICFC Ltd *(ICFC Ltd,* 91 Waterloo Road, London SE1 8XP; 01-928 7822).

Micro-electronics Applications Project: grants for awareness activities, courses, feasibility studies; *Department of Industry, MAP Information Centre,* 29 Bressenden Place, London SW1E 5DT; 01-213 3932.

Software Products Scheme: up to 50 per cent grant for innovative software; *National Computing Centre Ltd,* Oxford Road, Manchester M1 7ED; 061-228 6333.

Support for Innovation: up to 50 per cent grant for research and development. *RTP Division, Department of Industry,* 29 Bressenden Place, London SW1E 5DT; 01-213 5839.

Telecom Products Scheme: grants for developing products for attachment to Public Telecom networks; *Department of Industry, Information Technology Division,* Room 521, 29 Bressenden Place, London SW1E 5DT; 01-213 6505 or 6515.

Young Workers Scheme: leaflets from Jobcentres.

Exporting

Credit Risk Insurance: Export Credits Guarantee Department, Regional Office addresses from any British Overseas Trade Board number, or Small Firms Centre on freefone 2444 (via operator 100).

Export Marketing Research Scheme: grants of up to 50 per cent; *British Overseas Trade Board,* Export Marketing Research Section, 1 Victoria Street, London SW1H OET; 01-215 5277 (names A-I); 01-215 5282 (names J-Z).

Market Advisory Service: reports on prospects for selling particular products in specified markets and how to exploit them; *Department of Industry,* Regional Office telephone number from Small Firms Centre; freefone 2444 (via operator 100).

Market Entry Guarantee Scheme: grant of 50 per cent of cost of entering an overseas market; minimum costs £40,000. *Megs Unit,* 1 Victoria Street, London SW1H OET; 01-215 3157.

Statistics on Markets: Department of Trade, Statistics and Market Intelligence Library, 1 Victoria Street, London SW1H OET; 01-215 5444.

Status Reports on Overseas Agents: low-cost assessment of agents' capabilities; *British Overseas Trade Board, Overseas Status Section,* Sanctuary Buildings, 16-20 Great Smith Street, London SW1P 3DB; 01-215 3157.

Subsidised Overseas Exhibition Space: British Overseas Trade Board, Fairs and Promotions Branch, Dean Bradley House, 52 Horseferry Road, London SW1P 2AG; 01-212 7676.

Technical Help for Exporters, Linford Wood, Milton Keynes MK14 6LE; 0908 320033.

USEFUL ADDRESSES AND INFORMATION

Trade Opportunities: export intelligence service: British Overseas Trade Board, Lime Grove, Eastcote, Ruislip, Middlesex HA4 8SG; 01-866 8781 ext 265.

Appendix 5
Further Reading

People

The ABC of Interviewing, M Higham, Institute of Personnel Management (1979)
The Conduct of Meetings, Ed J Yelland, Kogan Page/Jordans (1983)
Croner's Reference Book for Employers, Croner's Publications Ltd, 173 Kingston Road, New Malden, Surrey KT3 3SS; 01-942 8966
Effective Interviewing for Employment Selection, C T Goodworth, Business Books (1979)
Employee Communications in the 1980s — A Personnel Manager's Guide, M Bland, Kogan Page (1980)
Employment Interviewing, J Munro Fraser, Macdonald & Evans (5th edn 1978)
Handbook of Personnel Management Practice, M Armstrong, Kogan Page (1977)
How to be your own Personnel Manager, P Humphrey, Institute of Personnel Management (1981)
How to Recruit, R Braithwaite and P Schofield, Gower (1979)

Planning and marketing

Be Your Own PR Man: A Public Relations Guide for the Small Businessman, Michael Bland, Kogan Page (1983)
Effective Marketing Management, C Kennedy and M Willis, Gower (1981, previously *Introduction to Marketing — the Cranfield Approach*, published by MCB Books)
Export for the Small Business, H Deschampsneufs, Kogan Page (1984)
Getting Sales: A Practical Guide to Getting More Sales for Your Business, R D Smith and G Dick, Kogan Page (1984)
Going International: The experience of smaller companies overseas, G D Newbould, P J Buckley and J Thurwell, Associated Business Press (1978)
How to Advertise, K Roman and J Mass, Kogan Page (1983)
Introducing Marketing, M Christopher, G Wills and M McDonald, Pan Books (1981)
Marketing, G B Giles, Macdonald & Evans (1978)
Marketing Management — Analysis, Planning and Control, P Kotler, Prentice-Hall International (4th edn 1980)
Principles of Marketing, P Kotler, Prentice-Hall International (1980)

Ways to expand

Acquisition and Corporate Development, J W Bradley and D H Horn, Lexington (1980)
Acquisitions and Mergers, J G Williams, ICAEW (1980)
Acquisitions of Private Companies, W L Knight, Oyez (1982)
Joint Ventures, E Herzfeld, Kogan Page/Jordans (1983)
Practical Corporate Planning, J Argenti, George Allen & Unwin (1980)
Taking up a Franchise, G Golzen, C Barrow and J Severn, Kogan Page (1983)

Law

The Company Director: his functions, powers and duties, P Loose, Kogan Page/Jordans (1983)
Company Law Materials 1, Kogan Page/Jordans (7th edn 1983)
Consumer Law for the Small Business, P Clayton, Kogan Page (1983)
International Trade: Essential Business Law, F Rose, Sweet & Maxwell (1979)
Law for the Retailer and Distributor, J R Lewis, Kogan Page/Jordans (3rd edn 1983)
Law for the Small Business: The Daily Telegraph Guide, P Clayton, Kogan Page (3rd edn 1983)
Reminders for Company Secretaries, J Birds, Kogan Page/Jordans (24th edn 1983)

Finance and control

An Insight into Management Accounting, J Sizer, Pelican Books (1980)
A Practical Approach to Financial Management, J Gibbs, Financial Training Publications (2nd edn 1980)
Business Finance, B Ogley, Longman (1982)
Cash Flow Management, J E Smith, Woodhead-Faulkner (2nd edn 1980)
Credit Management, R M V Bass, Business Books (1979)
Debt Collection Letters in Ten Languages, J Butterworth, Gower (1978)
Financial Management for the Small Business, C Barrow, Kogan Page (1984)
Financial Management Handbook, J E Broyles and I A Cooper, Gower (2nd edn 1981)
Introduction to Management Accounting, C T Horngren, Prentice-Hall International (5th edn 1981, previously *Accounting for Management Control*)
Managing Your Company's Finances, R Hargreaves and R Smith, Heinemann (1981)
Money for Business, Bank of England and City Communications Centre (1981)
Raising Finance: The Guardian Guide for the Small Business, C Woodcock, Kogan Page (1982)
Statistical Methods in Management, T Cass, Cassell (1969)
Successful Business Policies, G D Newbould and G A Luffman, Gower (1978)

SUCCESSFUL EXPANSION

Understand your Accounts, A St J Price, Kogan Page (1979)

General

Managing for Results, Peter F Drucker, Pan (1979)
The Effective Executive, Peter F Drucker, Pan (1970)
The Practice of Management, Peter F Drucker, Pan (1968)
Up The Organisation: how to stop the corporation from stifling people and strangling profits, Robert Townsend, Michael Joseph (1970)

Index

Accidents, *see* Safety
Accounting 52; aged debtors' list 58; books about 153-4; costing 53; credit control 57; invoicing 56; liquidity, working capital 18, 46, 49, 53, 55, 57, 111-21, 136-42; value added 54
Acts of Parliament, *see* Law
Advertising: job vacancies 31; publicity 82
Advice: use of 64, 67; sources of 70, 121, 148-51
After-sales service, *see* Customer service
Agricultural Development and Advisory Service (ADAS) 72
Analysis: production 123; product range 125-6
Attitudes: of owner 23; of staff 23-6, 28, 69-70; to work 22

Banks, banking 66, 115-17, 119-20
Biotechnology grants 149
Book list 152-4
Bonus, *see* Motivation
Borrowing 42, 46, 49
Bottleneck, *see* Limiting factor
Break even, *see* Planning, financial
British Overseas Trade Board (BOTB) 86, 150-51
British Technology Group 149
Budgets, *see* Planning
Business constitution, *see* Law
Business name, *see* Law
Buying, *see* Purchasing

Cash, *see* Accounting
Chambers of Commerce 73
Channels of distribution 45, 84-5
Collateral, *see* Security
Colleges 73, 103
Competitors 59, 60, 62, 90
Computer 15, 53, 57, 63; Aided Design/Manufacture Scheme 149
Conditions of work, *see* Environment for work
Consent *v.* coercion 37-8
Constitution of business, *see* Law

Consultants 16, 32, 47, 67-70; *see also* Advice, sources
Contract, *see* Law
Control: books on 153-4; management 14, 15, 18, 37, 39, 51-63, 79-80; production 128-9; stock 130; variety 125
Correlation, *see* Statistics
Costing, *see* Accounting, Planning
Council for Small Industries in Rural Areas (CoSIRA) 72, 103, 148, 149
Creative thinking 104-8
Credit control, *see* Accounting
Customer service 10-11, 59-60, 79, 84

Death 16, 21
De Bono, Dr Edward 104
Delegation 14, 18-19
Department of Trade and Industry 148-50
Distribution: channels of 45, 84-5; statistical 133-5

Efficiency 26, 35, 47
Employee: attitudes, *see* Attitudes; books on management of 152; car 40; clothes 40; health 15; ideas 15; key 33, 38, 44; reporting 39; responsibilities 30-31, 37, 44, 52; specification 31; strengths 15; stress 15
Energy Survey Scheme 149
Enterprise Agencies 71, 148
Environment for work 24, 28, 35
Equity 112, 118
European Coal and Steel Community 149
European Investment Bank 149
Export: Credits Guarantee Department 150; Market Advisory Service 150; Market Entry Guarantee Scheme 150; Market Intelligence Service 151; Market Research Scheme 150; status reports on agents 150
Exporting 85

155

SUCCESSFUL EXPANSION

Factory, *see* Premises
Fair treatment 29-30
Family: doctor 16; support 17
Federation of Microsystems Centres 148
Finance: appraisal 93-4, 113; books on 153-4; of customers 84-5; general 111-21, 136-42; houses 118; Government Loan Guarantee Scheme 6, 116, 150; of takeover 92, 95
Financial function 45
Fire, *see* Safety
Forecasts 42, 49; *see also* Planning
Franchising 108, 153
Function, product 123
Further reading 152-4

Government help 74, 103, 148-51
Grants 114, 132, 148-51

Herzberg, Frederick 28
Highlands and Islands Development Board 148

Illness 16, 21
Image 61, 132
Incentives, *see* Motivation
Industrial: psychology, *see* Psychology; robots 149; Tribunal, *see* Tribunal
Information, *see* Control
Insurance 16-17, 56, 117
Interviewing 32
Investor 118

Japan 40
Job description 30
Joint venture 109

Key employee 33, 38, 44

Labour and management attitudes 22
Law 30, 143-7
Lenders, *see* Borrowing
Limited companies 120, 143-4
Limiting factor 43, 122
Liquidity, *see* Accounting
Local authorities 71

Maintenance 131
Management: accounting 52-63, 136-42; effectiveness 124; job of 22, 44, 46, 47; labour attitudes 22; style 29
Marketing, markets 18, 75, 152
Marks & Spencer 11, 12, 124
Maslow, A H 27
McGregor, Douglas 27
Method of planning 44-6
Microelectronics Application Project 150
Monitoring, *see* Control
Motivation 33-5

Name of business, *see* Law

New customers 79, 81
New products 76-84, 98-110
Northern Ireland Development Agency 71, 148

Objectives, *see* Planning
Operating plans, *see* Planning
Order book 59, 60
Overdraft, *see* Banks
Overdue accounts, *see* Accounting
Overheads 45, 136-42
Owner: attitudes, *see* Attitudes; commitment 16; conscience 22; death 16; health 15; hours of work 14; illness 16; job of 14, 19, 38; responsibilities 18-19, 21-2, 36, 39; workload 19

Packaging 84, 106-7
Partnership 120, 143-4
Payback technique 93
People 21, 22; *see also* Employee
Performance monitoring, *see* Control
Planning: books on 152; budgets 53; financial 49, 53, 138-42; new products 102-3; objectives 40-44, 52; operational 48-9; research and development 74; strategic 40-48; takeover 89; work 39
Police 27, 30, 144
Polytechnics, *see* Colleges
Premises 131-2
Present value technique 93
Pricing 84, 98-100
Private investor 118
Probability, *see* Statistics
Product: appearance 84; specification 126-7
Production: capacity 47-8, 122; control and management 122-32; Engineering Research Association 74, 103, 148; staff and methods 34-5
Profit and loss accounts, budgets, *see* Accounting, Planning
Profitability 45, 59, 62
Psychology 26
Public companies 21, 24
Publicity 82
Purchasing 129-30

Quality 48, 54
Quality control 126-8

Reading list 152-4
Reasons for expanding 10, 13
Recruitment 30-33
Recruitment agency, consultant 31, 32
Regression, *see* Statistics
Reliability 12, 13, 127; *see also* Quality

INDEX

Reports 80, 129
Research and development 74; *see also* New products
Reservation of title 57, 147
Resources 46; inventory of 47
Return on investment 94-5
Robotics 25, 149

Safety 130-31
Sales 45; force 79-83; men 61; promotion 79, 82
Sampling, *see* Statistics
'Scientific management' 27
Scottish Development Agency 71, 148
Security: for borrowing 6, 116, 150; of information 67
Service, *see* Customer service
Small Firms Service 70, 114, 148
Small Firms Technical Enquiry Service 74
Software Products Scheme 150
Sole trader 120, 143
Solicitor 30, 121
Spouse 16, 17
Staff, *see* Employee
Statistics: book on 133, 153; export markets 150; in management 133-5; sampling 128, 133-5
Stock control, *see* Control
Strategy, business 41-50
Stress 15, 16, 21, 22

Style of management, *see* Management
Suppliers 59, 61, 144-7
Support for innovation 150
Systems, *see* Control

Takeover 88-97
Targets, *see* Planning
Taxation 97, 114, 120, 136-42
Technology Advisory Point 148
Telecom Products Scheme 150
Terms and conditions, *see* Law
Theories X and Y 27
Title, *see* Reservation of title
Tort, *see* Law
Tourist Boards 74
Tribunal 30, 39

Unfair dismissal 30
Universities, *see* Colleges

Value added, *see* Accounting
Variety control, *see* Control
VAT, *see* Taxation

Welsh Development Agency 71, 149
Work attitudes, *see* Attitudes
Work plans 39
Working conditions, *see* Environment for work
X, theory 27

Y, theory 27
Young Workers' Scheme 150